The History of Lea School

The History of Lea School

by

John Powell

John Powell

Logaston Press

This book is dedicated to the memory of
Lance Corporal Steven Gregory Sherwood
The Royal Gloucestershire, Berkshire and Wiltshire Light Infantry
8th April 1981 – 29th October 2005
who died in Afghanistan
and
All Pupils of Lea School who have lost their lives
in the Service of their Country

Logaston Press
Little Logaston Woonton Almeley
Herefordshire HR3 6QH
www.logastonpress.co.uk

First published by Logaston Press in 2010

ISBN 978 1 906663 42 1

Typeset in Minion Pro by Logaston Press
and printed in Great Britain by
Bell & Bain Ltd., Glasgow

Contents

Acknowledgements

The production of a new book always involves far more individuals than just the author and I owe thanks to many people: Mr. Ron Ablett, Mrs. Kath Ablett, Mrs. Pearl Ager, Mrs. E.E. Bevan, Mrs. K. Bevan, Mr. R. Bilby, Mr. Dick Brice, Mrs. Di Brice, Mr. Dick Cole, Mrs. J. Hatton, Mrs. Margaret Hay, Mr. Colin Howard, Miss Louise James, Mr. Alan Keef, Mrs. Peggy Luker, Mrs. M. Melhuish, the Rev. Neil Patterson, Mrs. Eunice Saunders MBE, Mr. Alan Sherwood, Mrs. Sue Sherwood, Mrs. Sue Thomas, Mrs. Linda Townsend, Mrs. Margaret Watson and Mrs. Sheila Williams. I am also indebted to: Mr. Rhys Griffith, Senior Archivist at Hereford Record Office; Mr. R.A. Robertson for allowing me to use his pen drawings of the school; Mr. Mike Carter for the use of family photographs; the late Mrs. Susan Keef (churchwarden) for her enthusiasm for this book and for allowing me to use records held at the church; and last, but not least, Andy and Karen at Logaston Press. If I have overlooked anyone, to them I sincerely apologise.

Author's Note

Soon after being appointed as head teacher of Lea School, I began to gather material for a junior-class project about the history of the village, and in the course of looking at census returns, tithe maps and their apportionment registers, church records and school log books, I decided that when time allowed, I would write a history of the school from its 19th-century beginnings to present times. A term or two later the class project went ahead but the school history was set aside because all the Victorian and early twentieth-century school log books were missing. I hoped that with luck they might have been deposited at the County Record Office or the Cathedral Library, but my enquiries in both Hereford and Gloucester came to nothing.

I appealed for information about them in the parish magazine and was quickly informed by Miss Gladys Davies, who became headmistress in 1935, that the complete set of log books from 1858 was in school when she retired in 1961. All subsequent searches for the books, however, including the contents of a mysterious, locked, black metal box in the church vestry, have proved to be utterly fruitless. I have therefore written this history without reference to them, so if they are ever discovered, it will fall to some future historian to revise what I have written, in the light of any new material they might provide.

In researching and writing this book I have been constantly reminded of the immense loyalty the school has sustained throughout its 150-year history. Indeed, it has attracted so many volunteer helpers and supporters over the years, that they are far too numerous to mention individually without overloading the text with names. To mention some and not others would almost inevitably leave some people feeling slighted, so, in order to avoid causing offence, I have restricted names very largely to those of members of staff, governors and members of the clergy.

There are, however, three former school friends of whom I wish to make particular mention: Sir John Paulson, for his constant interest and encouragement in the writing of this book and for his generosity in funding all the printing and publishing costs; and the late Mr. W.H. (Bill) Edwards and his wife, Mrs. Hilary Edwards, for giving so unstintingly of their time to answer myriads of questions and for happily sharing with me their memories and knowledge of Lea School both as pupils and governors. I am sincerely grateful to them all.

John Powell
Ross-on-Wye, February 2010

Sir John Paulson

*The late Bill Edwards
and Mrs Hilary Edwards*

Chapter 1
The Gift of Land

In the year 1858, just two days before Christmas, Maynard Colchester and his sisters, Helena, Henrietta, Dorothea and Arabella, all of The Wilderness, an impressive mansion in the Gloucestershire parish of Abenhall, paused in their festive preparations to sign an important document. It conveyed their gift of a half acre plot of land to the Curate Perpetual of Lea parish, its churchwardens and their successors, for the purposes of building a school and a residence for either a schoolmaster or a schoolmistress. The school was to provide education for 'poor persons of and in the said parish of Lea and other adjacent parishes and places ...'[1] and it was also stipulated that for the time being, the school should remain under the control and management of the Curate Perpetual, the Revd. William David Hall. It was, therefore, more than a little ironic that in the same year, 1858, the Crown assumed the government of India and, with British trade and shipping protected by the nation's supremely powerful Royal Navy, riches flowed into Britain from all corners of her enormous empire, but at home there was no state provision for education and the vast majority of Queen Victoria's subjects were illiterate. This had been a bone of contention ever since the passing of the Poor Law Amendment Act of 1834, because under the provisions of that Act, children in workhouses were supposed to receive three hours of instruction each day in reading, writing, arithmetic and the principles of the Christian religion. For the children of the independent poor, however, the only education available was that provided through charitable donations.

The truly enlightened had long fostered concerns about the lack of educational provision for the children of the poor, and during the eighteenth century a number of societies emerged to try to address the problem. The Society for the Promotion of Christian Knowledge (SPCK), founded in 1698, led the way and succeeded in building and maintaining many elementary schools throughout the country. Almost a century later, in the early 1780s, Robert Raikes of Gloucester began Sunday Schools and the idea was quickly adopted by both Anglicans and Dissenters alike. The monitorial system, generally credited to both Dr. Andrew Bell and Joseph Lancaster, started as an expedient in order to educate large numbers of children, but as the nineteenth century dawned it quickly became an accepted method of teaching. Under the system, an experienced teacher instructed adolescent monitors or monitoresses who then supervised groups of younger children and, with additional training and supervision, they might later achieve teacher status themselves. Joseph Lancaster's work in London was soon sponsored by prosperous Quakers and as a result of this association, the British and Foreign Schools Society was established in 1814. This society provided a religious education which was acceptable to Nonconformist groups because it was based on Bible readings and devoid of any dogma or doctrinal teaching.

At about the same time, members of the SPCK responded by founding the National Society for the Education of the Poor in the Principles of the Established Church throughout England and Wales. For practical purposes it was known simply as the National Society. It quickly assumed responsibility for the existing 230 SPCK schools and soon began to issue its own books and materials. It was not until 1833, however, that the government recognised the work of the two societies and assisted them with grants. The grants became a seriously contentious issue which generated enormous debate in parliament and in political circles generally, because many thought it perfectly reasonable that the Church of England should control religious education in schools. There were also those, of course, who saw dangers in providing education for the broad mass of the population; an educated mind was, after all, a questioning mind. Sadly, they had a vested interest in keeping the work force docile, accepting and unquestioning. Unfortunately, this was not in the best interests of the country, because in industry Britain led the world, and if that lead was to be sustained the working population needed, at the very least, a sound elementary education. State provision for a system of universal elementary education, however, did not begin until 1870 and even then arrangements were patchy and still poorly co-ordinated.

The Colchester family's generous donation of land for the building of Lea School in 1858 was therefore timely, and in advance of many other areas. It also showed a generosity of spirit, because at that time Maynard Colchester was the principal landowner in the parish and, although an Oxford-educated man himself, he could so easily have been

Former Lea Rectory (now a private dwelling)

Lea School and house (taken from school field)

one of those landlords who saw no good reason for the lower classes to learn to read and write. The previous lack of educational opportunities is revealed quite simply by a close look at the number of men and women who were unable to sign their names on their marriage certificates after the introduction of civil registration in 1836. A study of the marriage register for Lea Church indicates that of the first fifty marriages solemnised between 1837 and 1858, approximately half of both men and women were able to sign their names and the other half could only make a mark. When the first one hundred marriages were analysed, covering the years 1837 to 1891, then approximately two thirds of men and women could sign their names and only one third made their marks.

Despite the improvement, there was still much to do. It could not be denied that most gardeners, coachmen, miners, factory workers, waggoners, agricultural labourers, gamekeepers and domestic servants could perform their duties without any formal education at all, but this attitude condemned them to spend their whole lives in such occupations, with little or no chance of improving their personal standing or their material circumstances. It was no doubt convenient and advantageous for many employers to sustain and perpetuate this view and, surprisingly, they were aided and abetted to a very large extent, perhaps unwittingly, by the preaching of some very devout clergymen. In the first half of the nineteenth century in particular, clergymen often held strongly opposing views about the appropriateness of education for the poor, opinions which were frequently reflected in their church sermons. There were those who saw education as the only way for the poor to achieve self improvement and independence. Others took the opposite view, preaching that men and women should be content with their lot in life, however humble it might be. They argued that an individual's position in society was ordained by God and, that being so, any attempt to change it was against the law of God and should not be contemplated. It may be hoped, however, that some very wealthy clergymen were at times forced to wrestle with their consciences in reconciling their own personal interests as major landowners and their duties as guardians of their flock.

Many of the gentlemen who entered the Church of England ministry had previously lived privileged and financially secure lives in the sheltered atmosphere of Oxford colleges and understood little of life in the real world. Their futures were often assured; livings were frequently made available covertly through social connections or directly through their university colleges. In 1852, when the Revd. William David Hall began his ministry at Lea, the living was in the gift of the rector of Linton, and his living was in turn in the gift of St. John's College, Oxford. It was surely no coincidence that the incumbents of Linton, the Revd. Thomas Chandler Curties (1841-1865) and the Revd. Edward Palin (1865-1903) were both St. John's College men. The Revd. Hall was of Pembroke College, Oxford and the Lord of the Manor, Maynard Colchester, was a Magdalen College man. These Oxford connections were no doubt significant influences in clerical appointments and the furtherance of the teachings of the Established Church, and essential factors in the building of a school for the children of the Lea.

By the middle of the 1850s the Revd. Hall would have had ample time to get to know the local families, to understand the way of life in a small rural parish and, crucially, to assess its strengths and weaknesses. The lack of a school for the poor was one obvious weakness which needed to be remedied as soon as possible. Although no evidence has been discovered to prove that the Revd. Hall approached the Colchester family directly for a site, it seems quite likely that he did so, because they owned all the land surrounding the church and much more. The decision to build the school just across the road from Lea Church was clearly a very conscious one, to encourage communication between the two buildings in fostering church teachings. The parishioners were indeed fortunate in having the Revd. Hall as their priest because he clearly had no doubts about the importance of education for the poor in encouraging them to improve their personal circumstances by their own efforts. Unlike many other clergymen, he also had practical experience of the hardships of the world because, in addition to being a student at Pembroke College, Oxford and later a Fellow of New College, Oxford, he had spent the years 1841 to 1843 as a chaplain in the Royal Navy. When he and his wife, Julia, arrived at the Lea he was a mature young man of 36, a man who had seen much and was probably only too well aware of human fears and frailties. He was also an extremely generous man because, despite the sparse nature of available records, it seems certain that he paid for almost all of the building of Lea School out of his own pocket.

The original 1859 building plans do not appear to have survived, but evidence from a later survey suggests that they included provision for one large classroom attached to the schoolhouse and a separate block containing toilets and a coal house. The teaching

Lea Church (taken from school field)

of all the children from 5 to 14 years of age in one room, however, would have taxed the efficiency, the patience and the ingenuity of the most organised teacher, and it was probably to allow the infant children to be taught separately that a second, much smaller classroom was added in the 1870s. The evidence for this is found in a document signed by the Revd. Hall and his churchwardens, James Lodge and John James, in December 1873. They agreed that on receipt of a grant of ten pounds towards the building of a classroom, 'the said school shall always be in union with and conducted according to the principles and in furtherance of the ends and designs of the ... National Society'[2] – namely, the teachings of the Established Church.

The admissions register for the years 1859 to 1912 has long since disappeared, so it is difficult to know exactly how many children attended the school during that time, though trade directories for the period suggest that the average attendance was between 50 and 70 children. It is, however, possible to glean an impression of the children's families by studying the occupations of fathers on census returns and of husbands on marriage certificates. It might well be assumed that in a small rural parish occupations would very largely reflect the rural economy and the trades needed to sustain it, but there appears to have been a greater diversity of employment available than might have been expected. An analysis of the husbands' occupations recorded on the first one hundred marriage certificates issued for marriages solemnised at Lea Church between 1837 and 1891 revealed that there were three main groups: 22 were agricultural labourers; 24 described themselves as miners or colliers; and nine were farmers. The remaining 45 included a variety of traders, craftsmen, domestic servants and a few professional men and members of the clergy. They included: stonemasons, shoemakers, a saddler, a blacksmith, a tailor, grocers, a corn merchant, engine drivers, a clerk, a land agent, a chemist, clergymen, a stationmaster, a groom, a coachman and gardeners. It would seem likely, therefore, that the majority of the Lea School pupils would have been the children of gardeners, labourers, miners, traders, domestic servants, and some craft tradesmen.

Their lessons were, in the main, reading, writing and arithmetic and religious instruction, with considerable emphasis placed on acquiring a sound understanding and perfect recall of the catechism in readiness for confirmation as full members of the Church of England by the bishop. On cold, dreary days lessons would have proceeded slowly and ponderously because, although the classroom was heated by an open coal fire, there was no available source of artificial light. It is difficult to contemplate how well the children responded to the routines and disciplines of school, particularly the older ones who had been used to working on the land in all winds and weathers. It was common for them to begin their careers on the land at nine or ten years of age, so some no doubt found the school atmosphere restrictive and claustrophobic, and rebelled against it. Others, however, were probably content to be indoors – but of course not everyone could sit near the fire.

Chapter 2
Education for Heaven

Schoolmistresses were almost always spinsters or widows without dependants. Some were trained through the pupil teacher system, whilst others, often ladies of genteel upbringing but reduced circumstances, had to turn to teaching as a way of earning a living. Teaching provided them with reputable employment and a moderate regular salary. They were the obvious choice for charity schools because they were cheaper to employ; a schoolmaster required a higher salary since he was likely to have a wife and family to support. This attitude was not generally considered to be at all discriminatory: it was just seen as common sense. A single woman could live quite reasonably on a modest income and if she were to marry, it would then be her husband's duty to provide for her and she would be expected to give up her post in order make way for another single lady who had to support herself.

It was, however, not an easy way of life, particularly in rural areas where every move a single woman made would be observed and noted. As a teacher, she was in a position of trust and needed, at all costs, to show herself to be respectable and morally beyond reproach. It was a life which was heavily restricted and prescribed by parish expectations: church attendance two or three times every Sunday and perhaps an obligation to teach Sunday School too. As she lived almost directly opposite Lea Church, there is little doubt that schoolmistress Ellen Woodward would have had to conform to a similar pattern of life. The 1861 census described her as 24 years old, unmarried and a native of Somerset. She was, therefore, a long way from home and in need of the support, respect and approval of those around her, first and foremost the Revd. Hall and his wife at Lea Rectory.

The school house was an agreeable little residence with pleasant views across the fields. It had two bedrooms, a sitting room, a combined living room and kitchen, an outside lavatory, a well and a pump in the yard and quite a large garden but, like most houses at that time, it was probably difficult to heat to a reasonable degree of comfort. Anyone who recalls waking in an unheated bedroom with a cold face, ice on the inside of the windows and a frozen glass of water on the bedside table will be able to empathise with Miss Woodward. On dark winter mornings she must often have risen early and, candlestick in hand, have descended the steep, narrow stairs to the room below in the hope that the fire she had banked up with logs and slack coal the previous night could

Wynne and Felton SCHOOL.

RULES.

PARENTS ARE REQUESTED TO READ THESE RULES.

I.—Boys or Girls from the Parishes of Preston Wynne and Felton may attend this School.

II.—Each child (except those on Rev. H. T. Hill's list) to bring **Two Pence** every Monday Morning; no child will be admitted without the money; and when three are sent from one family, one of them to be *free*. Children of occupiers of farms in the Parish to pay 4d. weekly.

III.—School hours from 9 to 12, and from 2 to 5, in the Summer half-year; and from 2 to 4 in the Winter half-year.

IV.—The attendance to be regular and punctual, and the pence to be paid for each week in which children have NO LEAVE to be absent.

V.—Holidays will be allowed at Christmas, during Corn Harvest, and during Hop-picking; and every Saturday will be a Holiday.

VI.—Children will be expected to attend the Sunday Schools in their respective Parishes.

VII.—Children absent from School without leave will, after three weeks, be crossed off the Books.

VIII.—Children to come to School NEAT and CLEAN.

IX.—If Parents have any cause for complaint, they should apply to the *Clergyman* of the Parish.

X.—No Children will be admitted under Five or above Fourteen years of age, and only on Monday mornings at NINE o'clock. Parents to *bring them*.

.XI.—Girls are to bring their own work on Mondays and Tuesdays, and to do work provided for them on Wednesdays, Thursdays, & Fridays.

XII.—Children to pay for their own Copy Books; all other books provided.

" Education is the Training Immortal Souls for Heaven."

be stirred into life to heat a kettle of water for tea, whilst she unlocked the kitchen door and picked her way across icy flagstones to stir the classroom fire into action. With luck, she could have rekindled it quite quickly, but if it had burnt out overnight then the ashes would have to be raked out and carried away and a new fire started in readiness for morning lessons. The original classroom was a large room with a lofty ceiling and even if the coal fire was effective, it was unlikely to warm all parts of the room adequately by the start of morning lessons at 9 o'clock. In some cases, children would have walked two or three miles to school, perhaps poorly clothed and inadequately shod for bad weather, so they would have arrived cold, wet and uncomfortable. Despite the ineffectiveness of the coal fire and the trials it must have caused the schoolmistress in the cold hours of early morning, to the children it must have been extremely important.

Although the Revd. Hall enjoyed complete autonomy in the management of Lea School at that time, the general organisation was probably quite similar to that of other small church schools. In that respect, a useful impression may be drawn from the administration of the school built for the children of the equally rural parishes of Preston Wynne and Felton, near Bromyard, where the Revd. R.T. Hill appears to have occupied a similar position. Parents were presented with a printed sheet of attendance rules which, for the few who could actually read them, were simple, direct and demanding. The school was open to boys and girls between the ages of 5 and 14 who lived in the parishes of Preston Wynne and Felton, where they must also attend Sunday School. New entrants were admitted at 9 o'clock on Mondays only, and on condition that they were accompanied by parents. The children of farmers were charged 4d per week. All other children had to pay 2d per week, with the exception of the third child of a family and those children on the Revd. Hill's list, who were allowed to attend school free of charge. The fees for these children were probably met from a separate charitable fund or, quite possibly, paid by the clergyman himself.

The hours of attendance were long compared with those of modern times: from 9 to 12 each morning, and from 2 to 5 in the summer and 2 to 4 in the winter. The children were expected to be clean, neat in appearance, punctual and regular in their attendance. Once the fees had been paid on Monday morning they had no leave of absence, and any child who was absent for three weeks or more, whatever the cause, had his or her name removed from the school register. All books were provided free of charge except copy books, which had to be paid for by the families. Curiously, girls had to bring their own work, usually needlework, on Mondays and Tuesdays, but were given tasks set by the teacher on the other days of the week. Holidays were allowed on Saturdays, at Christmas, and during hop-picking and the corn harvest; child labour was important in rural areas at certain times of the year and education was set aside whilst essential work was completed. Many parents were probably not greatly concerned about this, because the earnings from field work done by the older children provided a much needed addition to the household income. If parents had cause for complaint about any aspect of their children's schooling, they were directed to take their concern to their own parish clergyman who would investigate the matter. Church schools existed essentially to convey the teachings of the Church of England – that is, they were in pursuit of high standards of morality and unblemished reputations. As if to reinforce this point, at the end of the school rules was the ominous, slightly menacing caption: 'Education is the Training (of) Immortal Souls for Heaven'. In that respect, the schools over which the Revd. Hall and the Revd. Hill presided were almost certainly very similar in outlook, aims and the nature of their organisation. The children would probably have spent much of their lesson time learning by rote because, without artificial light, on dark dreary days it would have been the only practical way to work. Multiplication tables could be practised and the questions and responses of the catechism could be perfected while the children sat in a numbing gloom, relieved only by the flickering of the fire and the wavering flame of the candle on the teacher's reading desk.

The Revised Code of 1862 doubtless brought Miss Woodward and her pupils some practical improvements and, hopefully, additional comforts, but it was a double-edged sword in that it consolidated government thinking about payment by results. The receipt of annual government grants depended on inspectors writing satisfactory reports about the adequacy of school buildings, the calibre of the teachers and the general progress of the children's learning. Buildings had to have good drainage and appropriate sanitary arrangements. Classrooms had to have good lighting and ventilation and provide a prescribed amount of space for each child. The children had to be grouped into six standards according to age, and precise attainments in reading, writing and arithmetic were prescribed for each age group. Inspectors made annual visits to test the children to see if they had attained a level appropriate to their age group and standard. For standards III to VI the reading test meant the sight reading of given passages of varying difficulty; taking dictation from the same or similar passages answered for the writing test; and arithmetic was tested through the children's knowledge of the four rules of number– addition, subtraction, division and multiplication – and their application to problem solving. The school's grant for the next year was calculated on the basis of each child's performance in each subject. It is little wonder, therefore, that children spent much of their time taking dictation and learning things by heart. The Revised Code also stipulated that the girls must receive weekly instruction in needlework, which perhaps explains the rule that girls had to bring their own work to school on Mondays and Tuesdays.

In addition to the testing of children, there was also increased scrutiny of the teaching staff and the level of their training and qualifications. The head teacher now had to hold a teacher's certificate and the school also had to comply with various rules and conditions with regard to the number of pupil teachers and assistant teachers who comprised the staff. It is questionable, therefore, whether Miss Woodward and her contemporaries considered payment by results as entirely beneficial to their pupils or to themselves. It is of course impossible to know exactly how individual teachers of that time might have reacted, but it is reasonable to suppose, without too much conjecture, that some viewed the Revised Code much as modern teachers have viewed the implementation of the National Curriculum; that is, rather like the curate's egg, good in parts.

Throughout the 1860s the drive to provide elementary schools continued to proceed on parallel lines, the two lines being Church of England schools and Nonconformist

Lea Church

schools. Competition between the two groups remained vigorous because neither wanted the other to have greater influence over religious teaching in schools than itself. Unfortunately, they were both struggling to keep pace with the demand created by a burgeoning population. In the first half of the nineteenth century the population of England and Wales had doubled, increasing from just under nine million in 1801 to just under eighteen million in 1851, and it was showing no signs of slowing down. This was of particular concern to the Nonconformists because if the state intervened to provide the additional schools needed, the independence of their own schools might be undermined. They were fearful that the government might attempt to impose one uniform system of elementary education on everyone, a system which would almost certainly embrace the teachings of the Church of England, leaving the Nonconformists with little control over the religious education of their own children.

The state eventually intervened with the Education Act of 1870. There still exists a generally held view that the 1870 Act brought about universal elementary education that was both compulsory and free; it did not. Its provisions helped to make school places available for all, but universal compulsory attendance and the abolition of fees were still some years away. The 1870 Act gave powers to local town councils and rural church vestries to elect Boards of Education to build and manage elementary schools in areas where no other schools existed or where the number of places was inadequate. It also allowed them to make their own decisions about the nature of religious instruction, with the safeguard that no attempt should be made to guide children to any particular denomination. For the most part they were nondenominational, the religious teaching being provided through Bible readings with explanations in terms of general morality. The Board Schools just filled the gaps in existing provision, and the dual system which evolved allowed the government to achieve its aims without creating religious turmoil. The provision of elementary school education gradually covered all of England and Wales, the churches were able to continue as before, and much of the expense continued to be met by religious charities. It is for these reasons that Lea School and many village schools in the district have remained Church of England Aided Schools into the twenty-first century.

Chapter Three
School Versus Work

In the 1870s the headmistress of Lea School was Mary Ann Lambeth, a 33-year-old spinster from Liverpool. Lea must have seemed like another world compared with a large bustling city, and one wonders how she adjusted to life in a very rural parish where, at certain times of the year, work in the fields took preference over lessons in school. For a dedicated teacher, intent on doing her best for her pupils, it must have been very disheartening to see their progress lapse, or wither totally, as a result of weeks spent doing agricultural work. In small village schools there was often a high turnover of teaching staff and it is more than likely that this resulted from poor working conditions, frequent pupil absences, and the unrelenting pressures generated by the system of payment by results. Government grants depended on results – results which some teachers clearly saw as unachievable with such poor pupil attendance. It seems likely, however, that Miss Lambeth was well regarded and fairly happy in her position, because records indicate that she remained at Lea School for at least seven years.

Although the 1870 Act helped to provide elementary school places in areas where hitherto they had been lacking, issues surrounding school attendance rumbled on for another generation. In that time a myriad of acts, codes and regulations, too numerous and too tedious to be included here, were introduced, but still no uniform system of elementary education existed, because Board School regulations did not apply to denominational schools and there were numerous loopholes which parents could exploit in order to send their older children to work rather than to school. It must also be remembered that not all parents were convinced of the need for their children to be educated, particularly if they had received no education themselves. Children were kept away from school for many reasons: poor health, severe weather, parents' inability to pay fees, and, of course, due to the need for agricultural labour.

Health was a particular issue because there were frequent outbreaks of measles, mumps, chickenpox, whooping cough, scarlatina, influenza, smallpox and diphtheria, which occasionally resulted in schools being closed for weeks at a time in order to curtail the spread of these illnesses. There were also difficult situations when children were sometimes sent home from school because they had head lice or because they were generally dirty and suffering from scabies, the highly contagious skin disease generally known then as the 'itch', which appeared and spread through poor hygiene. When schoolmasters and schoolmistresses made attempts to enforce cleanliness, however, parents who were unaware of their own poor standards of hygiene felt insulted and became hostile. They appeared to take the view that their personal cleanliness was none of the school's business, even though it might have quite serious consequences for the health of other pupils. Severe weather also took its toll on health and school attendance, particularly during prolonged wet spells when footpaths were turned into impassable quagmires and roads became flooded. Those children who did set out to walk to school often arrived soaked to the skin because they had inadequate clothes and boots, and after being given a warm drink, they were often sent home again.

The main reason for pupil absences, however, was the demand for child labour in the fields. To be fair to the parents, they frequently had little choice in the matter, not least because most of them lived in tied cottages. In spring there was potato-setting, bark-stripping and crow-scaring, and a little later came haymaking and the singling of turnips. Schools closed for six weeks in the summer for holidays which were described very precisely as 'Harvest Holidays' and the older boys were often retained into September to follow the reapers to bind the sheaves of corn. As the autumn progressed, they were required to assist with the apple harvest and then the backbreaking labour of turnip-pulling and the picking up of potatoes. If a farmer made it clear to his workmen that their sons were needed to help with any of these tasks, or the lord of the manor asked for them to beat covers for his pheasant shoots in November and December, it was very difficult for them to refuse and send the boys to school. Also, when the boys were absent from school for a week or two, the parents could save the school fees and the boys themselves would receive some earnings for their efforts, even if

Lea School Victorian building – probably late 1870s or 1880s

payment was received partly in kind. Similarly, the older girls in a family were often kept at home to look after younger brothers and sisters if their mother was needed to help with the additional domestic work generated at the 'big house' during shooting parties or other festivities. Landowners and farmers tended to view these activities as unwritten obligations or rights which came with their providing their workers with permanent employment. The reality was that the interests of the higher echelons of the rural community came first, and disruption to the village children's education was not of prime concern.

It was almost inevitable, therefore, that even when parents were keen for their children to attend school regularly, their lessons often fell victim to the maintenance of vested interests against which the parents could not contend. They could not afford to be at odds with their employers over the issue of child labour for fear of losing their jobs and their homes. The stark reality of the situation was that access to education continued to depend very largely on social status. The protection of the social hierarchy did, however, cause serious conflicts of interest for some employers, because the landowners and tenant farmers who so often sought the labour of children in their fields were also the men who sat on school management boards, whose duty it was to encourage regular pupil attendance. The children and their parents were pawns in a cynical game of manipulation and inevitably the parents took the blame for their children's irregular attendance at school and general lack of progress in reading, writing and arithmetic.

This point was illustrated in May 1874, when, having praised the efforts and good work of the schoolmistress, one of Her Majesty's Inspectors wrote in the log book of a local school as follows: 'The school now gives promise of better things, but parents should understand that if they keep away their children, as they have hitherto done, no teacher worth having will ever stay at this school.'[1] Teachers were in as invidious a position as the parents and could quite easily find themselves being made scapegoats when things went wrong. If government grants were denied because the annual inspection had revealed deficiencies in the children's progress, it would certainly be said to be the teacher's fault, and of course no blame could possibly accrue to the members of the school board on whose land the children had been working whilst they should have been in lessons. The fact that Miss Lambeth remained at Lea School for some years, however, suggests that she was well respected and that the attendance of her pupils during the 1870s was fairly reasonable.

In small rural communities, where social status tended to be measured in terms of wealth and the possession of land, the social status of schoolmistresses such as Miss Lambeth remained a little uncertain because, although they were much better educated than most of the inhabitants, this was counteracted by their lack of worldly wealth. Those parents who appreciated the teachers' efforts to educate their children almost certainly treated them with great respect, while those less convinced of the need for their children to go to school probably granted them a grudging respect because of their position. The highly prosperous but semi-literate tenant farmers of the parish, however, were likely to consider teachers as little more than servants.

These social attitudes were clearly revealed in the way that church seats were assigned to parishioners with widely differing incomes and influence. At the Lea, church seats could be reserved on payment of an annual fee which, in the 1870s, appears to have ranged from 5 shillings to 40 shillings a year, but how these sums were arrived at remains unclear. What *is* clear is that if payments lapsed the churchwardens lost no time in declaring the seats to be 'free and unappropriated' and starting to look for an alternative fee payer. The location of seats appears to have depended as much on a person's perceived social status as on his or her ability to pay the fee. Farmers tended to assume that the ownership or occupation of a particular farm assured them of a seat in church which accorded with their social standing in the parish. In many cases seats were allocated as much to properties as to people, so preserving an image of the parish's social hierarchy in church even when properties changed hands. All of the parishioners were expected to know and, most importantly, accept their place in the social hierarchy. This elitist and rather deferential attitude was confirmed by the very precise wording of the decisions recorded in the vestry minutes of Lea Church, which reflect the accepted social expectations of the time. In August 1874 the vestry clerk, probably wheelwright and carpenter Henry James, recorded that: 'The churchwardens have assigned to Mr. Charles Yemm as tenant of New House Farm, the 3rd seat from the pulpit in the nave of the Lea Church for the use of himself and family,[2] and in April 1875 he minuted that they had 'assigned to Mr.

Linton Church

16

Lea Church

William Bennett as tenant of Norton Farm, the 2nd seat on the south side of the nave for the use of himself and family.'[3] In both cases these men were provided with seats near the front of the church as a recognition of their social standing in the community as tenants of particular farms and, crucially, as men who provided employment and income for agricultural labourers and were therefore seen as masters of men.

Thus it was that those landowners and farmers holding the largest acreages had the best seats for observing the ritual of the service and the best opportunity to hear their priest. Next came the owners or tenants of smaller farms, followed by smallholders, then cottagers, and finally the labourers and the poor. The social structure of the parish was reinforced even at prayer. It is unfortunate that no seating plan for Lea Church has survived, but a plan for Linton Church dated 1839 has been preserved and it clearly indicates the thinking of the vicar and churchwardens who constructed it. It confirms that the position of a family pew in that church was indeed commensurate with property and social standing. One pew was allocated to the occupant of Linton School House, but being just three pews from the back of the church it was almost as far from the communion table and the pulpit as it could possibly be, and says much about the standing in Linton's community of their humble schoolmistress and the attitudes of its clergy, churchwardens and most prominent inhabitants. No doubt they saw themselves as good Christians and intended that their own children should be brought up in the same manner, but their attitude to their schoolmistress appears to have been rather curious and not a little hypocritical. After their parish priest she was the parishioner with the greatest influence over religious instruction and the promotion of the church's teaching but despite her important role in the community, she was only worthy of a seat at the back of the church. In

1854, Lea Church was completely restored and renovated, and probably remains much as Victorian congregations would have known it. Readers who know Lea Church and are familiar with its present seating plan might pause to wonder where the schoolmistress of Lea School, Miss Mary Ann Lambeth, might have been permitted to sit.

Chapter Four
Compulsory Education

In 1877, Queen Victoria was declared Empress of India. Her vast empire, of which India was considered to be 'The Jewel in the Crown', was approaching the zenith of its power, influence and wealth, and Great Britain was the richest country in Europe and possibly the world. Yet despite this incredible wealth, children in parishes up and down the country continued to take pennies to school each Monday morning to pay for their lessons – pennies many parents struggled to find. As the 1870s drew to a close, school fees and school attendance continued to be contentious issues and the organisation and funding of elementary education remained confused and uneven. There had been more Education Acts since 1870 and numerous changes in regulations, but anything resembling a truly national system was still many years away. Elementary education would always be inefficient and lack cohesion until attendance was compulsory for all, but that battle was yet to be won.

School attendance continued to be unsatisfactory. Attempts to address the problem were thwarted to some extent because the administrative powers available to schools were not uniform. Under the 1870 Act, Board Schools had been given powers to make attendance compulsory in their particular districts by framing their own by-laws. Parents who ignored attendance orders without very good reason could be taken to court and fined up to 5 shillings, a large sum for men earning little more than 10 to 15 shillings per week. Very few Boards, however, actually availed themselves of these powers, perhaps seeing them as a double-edged sword. If they used their powers and applied them firmly, they might appear to be very dogmatic compared with the voluntary schools to whom such powers were not available. They might, as it were, win skirmishes with a few very awkward families, but ultimately lose the battle to convince the majority of parents of the importance of education. This was clearly a ridiculous situation, so in districts where School Boards did not exist, voluntary schools were given the same powers through the introduction of School Attendance Committees. These powers were made legally binding on both agencies through Mundella's Act of 1880 and it seemed that the vexed problem of compulsory elementary education was, on paper, finally settled. The reality, however, was rather different.

Mundella's Act was devised, drafted and passed by city dwellers, perhaps largely with city dwellers in mind and little appreciation of the practical concerns of people living in the countryside. It will be remembered from Chapter 1 that the deed granting the gift of land for the site of Lea School stipulated that as well as providing education for the poor of Lea parish, children from adjacent parishes should be allowed admission too. This was a very flexible, common-sense approach; no doubt, the Colchester family and the Revd. Hall intended it to be so in order to encourage school attendance, irrespective of where children lived. They could attend the school most convenient for them without attracting any of the catchment-area intrigues and disputes which so plagued and frustrated head teachers and school governors a century or so later. It is likely, therefore, that as well as taking children from the immediate vicinity of the village, Lea School admitted children from areas as far away as Eccleswall Farm, Wharton Farm, Norton Farm, Lea Line, Knightshill Farm and Warren Farm. To walk these distances the children would have had to set out early and, in winter, perhaps arrive home at dusk or in darkness. In the summer months and in good weather these journeys were possible: in winter months, however, during spells of severe weather sensible parents would have kept their children at home for the good of their health.

The inhabitants of Lea parish may have thought that the industrial revolution had passed them by, and in many respects perhaps it had, but not completely, because the recent establishment of the railway station provided hitherto unimaginable social and economic opportunities for those able to make good use of the railways. The rail connection made the parish far less isolated than in former times, and open to a wider world. As the rail network grew throughout the country, and more and more transactions and messages had to be recorded, increasing numbers of its employees needed to be able to read and write accurately, not least the station master. The enumerator of the Lea census for 1881 recorded the occupants of the station master's house as Edwin Manaton, his wife, Alice, and their five young children. Signalman Henry Chamberlain and his wife, Mary, both in their twenties, lived at Lea Line; and porter Charles Boroughs and his wife, Elizabeth, also in their twenties, appear to have been sharing the school house with the new 22-year-old schoolmistress, Miss Mary Rosser. It could not be denied that England was in the midst of great change. The need for improved standards of education amongst the general population would very soon become vital for future progress and could not be ignored, but many had still to be convinced.

Throughout the 1880s and 1890s there were numerous cases in which parents were brought before the courts for failing to send their children to school. Some were fined sums ranging from 2 to 5 shillings, but others escaped with a caution. On the last day of March 1883, the final day of the school year in Victorian times, one local headmaster wrote despairingly of a year of continual strife between the School Board and the parents, one group endeavouring to get the children into school and the other keeping them away to work in gardens, fields and their own homes. He added: 'In the case of those who have been summoned before the magistrates the Board have failed to obtain support, judgement going against them.'[1] Even when court appearances secured a conviction, it seems to have had little effect, for in June the following year he wrote: 'I am sorry to say that the attendance is very irregular, although several of the parents were fined at Harewood End (Petty Sessions) on Monday last.'[2]

Lord Sandon's Act of 1876 had forbidden the employment of children under 10 years of age and children between 10 ad 14 were required to attend school half-time, but it is clear that these provisions were often ignored. In 1893 the school leaving age was raised to 11, but in some cases this appears to have meant little to parents or employers. In May 1896, another local headmaster noted disconsolately in his log book the names of two boys who should have been in school but were actually working for two of the school managers. The hypocrisy of such men must have been extremely demoralising for the headmaster, who knew that his efforts were being undermined by the very people who were supposed to uphold the law and enforce school attendance. To add insult to injury, it must have been particularly galling to have to accept that there was probably nothing he could do about it. The landowners' interests continued to come first. In June 1896 the same headmaster wrote with obvious anger and frustration that one of the boys in his class was absent yet again and working for the blacksmith at Crowhill. He concluded angrily that: 'This boy is an habitual truant, and although I have reported him scores of times to the Schools Attendance Officer, no notice is taken'.[3] It would appear that there was, almost certainly, collusion in the acceptance of child labour at many levels. In 1899 the school leaving age was raised to 12, but there were always going to be parents who ignored attendance orders and probably court orders as well.

Attitudes towards the problem of school fees were both muddled and unrealistic. School log books provide clear evidence that teachers found it difficult to collect the weekly fees from parents in farming areas because of the high levels of rural poverty which resulted from large families, low wages and seasonal unemployment. Parents who could not afford the fees could seek assistance from the Poor Law Guardians,

Lea School 1910

but many would have been reluctant to do so for fear of being considered paupers by their neighbours. It should come as no surprise, therefore, that education was not the parents' prime concern, their main priority being to boost their earnings to provide their family with food and clothes. In considering the arguments for compulsory elementary education it is easy to forget the crushing drudgery of daily existence in the nineteenth century. Many farm workers were worn out long before their time and lived in fear of ending their days in the workhouse – for Lea parishioners, the imposing and prison-like building in Alton Street, Ross, where the community hospital now stands. The rosy picture of life in the countryside so beloved of sentimental Victorian artists was far from the truth. It belied the fact that life at work and at home was labour-intensive, arduous and exhausting. It is little wonder that some children arrived at school unwashed and in dirty clothes, particularly when water had to be drawn from wells or collected from springs and carried in heavy buckets long distances across fields. Keeping the older children at home to help with chores must have been very tempting, and almost certainly a necessity when little brothers and sisters were ill with childhood diseases such as measles and chickenpox, or when the arrival of another child was imminent. Mundella's Act, if they knew about it, would have been the least of their concerns. In 1891, however, parents were given the right to demand free education for their children and as a result most schools gave up the struggle to collect pennies and lessons became free. No doubt it was a great relief to all concerned.

Kelly's Trade Directory for Herefordshire in 1885 listed the National School headmistress as a Mrs. King, and in the 1891 census the occupants of the school house at Lea were schoolmistress Elizabeth King, a 47-year-old widow and her 15-year-old niece, Elizabeth Watkins, who was a school monitress and would have worked under her aunt's instruction. A decade later, in 1901, they were still at the school, and Elizabeth Watkins was then described as an assistant mistress. They must have given good account of themselves and met with the approval of the vicar, the school managers and the community, because there would have been little likelihood of their having remained in post for so long if they had been found wanting. In many rural schools there was a high turn over of teaching staff, possibly exacerbated by attendance issues, so the lengthy stay of these ladies at Lea would have been very good for the school in maintaining continuity and stability. Their tenure of over a decade and that of their predecessor, Miss Mary Lambeth, also suggests, without too much conjecture, that attendance at the school was generally fairly good and that they found their working conditions agreeable.

During the 1890s the government exerted greater influence over elementary education, and this resulted in the widening of the curriculum to include subjects beyond the three Rs and religious instruction. In Church of England schools, however, religious instruction and the learning of the catechism in preparation for confirmation by the bishop remained fundamental to school life. Inspectors from the diocese made regular visits to schools and their reports appear to have been fair and generally positive in nature. Heavy criticism, of course, would have been damning not only of the school-

Lea Handbell Ringers (1897/8) with the Revd. H. Hodson. Miss Sybil Havergal of Castle End House is centre front, and immediately behind her is Mr. Harry Rudge, who played the violin at church socials.
(By kind permission of Mrs. H. Edwards)

master or schoolmistress, but of the vicar too, because it was generally expected that he would visit the school on a weekly basis in order to supervise religious instruction and ensure that the church's teachings were given appropriate respect. Given his sustained interest in Lea school over many years, there can be little doubt that the Revd. Hall was diligent in this regard. Although the Revd. Hall and many other similarly open-minded and generous people throughout the land did much to provide educational opportunities for the masses by donating land and money for the building of schools and by giving generously of their time to ensure that building projects were brought to successful conclusions, as the nineteenth century drew to a close the provision of elementary education remained muddled and incoherent. A well co-ordinated national system of education was still some years away, though progress had been made in the years since Lea School was founded.

The people of Lea had indeed been very fortunate when, in 1852, the Revd. William David Hall accepted the living and came to live amongst them. He remained the guardian of the flock for 27 years, a generation, and quite possibly officiated at the marriages of infants he had christened and children he had taught in scripture lessons at Lea School. He relinquished the living in 1879 and settled for the last ten years of his life at Abenhall. The evidence of his signature in the church registers indicates, however, that he still sometimes officiated at Lea services and perhaps kept an eye on the school he had nurtured for so many years. He obviously retained a lasting affection for the parish, for he chose it for his last resting place – so perhaps he watches there still.

The Revd. Hall was clearly an enlightened man. Through his foresight, hard work and generosity a school was provided for the children of the poor of Lea, and under his guidance it seems to have flourished. As the long Victorian era was drawing to a close, however, social attitudes seem to have changed very little with regard to the status of the children in his school. In April 1897, the vestry clerk was directed to minute that the vestry wished it to be placed on record that since definite seats had been allotted to the school children, they should not be exceeded, because additional encroachments resulted in complaints from other parishioners. The vestry hoped 'that calling attention to this matter will prevent further inroad upon other seats reserved for the general congregation'.[4] One wonders how the Revd. Hall might have reacted to such comments: they seem to have suggested that the children of the National School and, indirectly, perhaps their teachers too, should know their place and keep to it.

Chapter 5
Changing Times

Queen Victoria died at Osborne House on the Isle of Wight in January 1901, and the news of her passing cast a heavy gloom over the whole kingdom. In cities, towns and villages throughout the land headmasters and headmistresses gathered their charges together in their school rooms to inform them of the nation's great loss, and there can be little doubt that Mrs. Elizabeth King also did her duty at Lea School. The news soon travelled to the queen's relatives in Germany, Denmark, Norway and Russia and in due course reached the furthest outposts of the Empire. The long Victorian era (1837-1901) had passed, and the world would never be quite the same again.

The world was indeed changing. Ever since the late 1880s British politicians had been increasingly aware of the rising power of France, Germany and Russia and the threat they might pose to Britain and her Empire in future times. Competition in international trade was becoming more challenging and Britain could no longer assume world naval supremacy. As the new century dawned the British Empire and its contribution to Britain's military and economic interests needed to be reassessed. Politicians planned a future in which Britain would provide the Empire with manufactured goods, administrators and finance for development, and in return the Empire would provide Britain with food and, in times of danger, manpower. It was crucial, therefore, that the general public, particularly the nation's youth, should understand Britain's relationship with the Empire, because it was assumed that young men and women who emigrated to Canada, Australia and New Zealand would retain a natural allegiance to Britain. In order to emphasise the Empire's importance to Britain's survival in changing times, its history and geography were taught in glowing terms and elementary schools were allowed to close each year to celebrate Empire Day, the 24th May, Queen Victoria's birthday.

King Edward VII was crowned in June 1902, and schools closed for a week's 'Coronation Holiday'. Life soon returned to normal, however, once the excitement of the coronation and the celebration bonfires had died down, and teachers in country schools continued to wrestle with the enduring problem of poor attendance. School log books of the time indicate that the reasons for poor attendance had not changed: severe weather, inadequate attire and the inevitable and frequent outbreaks of measles, mumps, chickenpox, whooping cough, scarlet fever and diphtheria which often resulted in local schools being closed for weeks at a time on the orders of the Medical Officer of Ross

A class at Lea School in the early 20th century
(By kind permission of Mrs. H. Edwards)

Poor Law Union. Work in the fields also continued to take its toll, and headmasters and headmistresses continued to complain to Attendance Officers. Their attempts to obtain warrants to bring parents to court were, however, frequently frustrated by the influence of the landowners who employed the children, some of whom almost certainly sat on school management boards and as local magistrates too. Added to all this, most parents needed every penny their children could earn, and many of them simply remained blind to the benefits of education. They appear to have accepted that their sons would spend their lives working on the land, often on the same farms as previous generations of their family. They also seem to have been conditioned to accept that their daughters would go into domestic service until they were married and set up their own homes. Indeed, it was not uncommon for country house ladies to visit village schools to inspect the girls' sewing in order to assess their suitability for employment.

Although there had been some widening of the elementary school curriculum to include history, geography and natural science, the emphasis was still very much on the three Rs and religious instruction. The church remained steadfast in support of its schools; and the schools continued to uphold the church's teachings and to observe the main religious festivals including services in church on Ash Wednesday and Ascension Day. The children's understanding of religious knowledge was examined each year by diocesan inspectors, and the rector or vicar visited the school each week to oversee the older pupils' preparation for confirmation. In 1900, the living at Lea had been presented to the Revd. Charles Lewis Cator Buee. The first census of the new century, in 1901, recorded that he was then aged 33, and his household included his wife Geraldine, aged 35, their three children and two female servants. Indeed, as the new reign began the old structures of rural society remained largely unchanged and no doubt life in most villages, including Lea and its neighbours, continued to revolve round the church, the school, the seasons and agriculture.

The reign of Edward VII has often been described as the 'Long Garden Party' because of the king's enjoyment of glittering spectacle and splendour, which had, in truth, come as a welcome relief from the gloomy and oppressive atmosphere at Court in the last years of Queen Victoria's reign. Edward certainly liked to enjoy himself and lived life to the full, so much so that the enduring picture of him in the public memory is merely that of a playboy, but such a view is neither accurate nor fair. Combined with his generally affable nature and his colourful character came natural diplomatic skills which he often

The Revd. C.L.C. Buee (rector 1900-1923)
(By kind permission of Mrs. H. Edwards)

employed as peacemaker amongst the crowned heads of Europe, many of whom were his relatives. As king of England and head of a vast Empire he could speak with authority, even to his nephew Kaiser Wilhelm II of Germany, but his passing in May 1910 left a diplomatic void amongst Queen Victoria's many descendants and family connections. By 1910 the old order in Europe was changing, and difficult times lay ahead for king and country.

In June 1909, there were changes at Lea School. Mrs. Elizabeth King relinquished her post as headmistress, most probably to retire. She had served the school for a quarter of a century, which suggests that she was happy in her work and well respected by parishioners. She had been assisted for many years, at least since 1891, by her niece, Miss Elizabeth Watkins, first as a school monitress and later as a qualified teacher. It is unclear when Miss Watkins left, but she appears to have remained at her post for several years to assist the new headmistress, Mrs. A.J. Edkins. In retirement she took rooms at Westlea with Miss Lucy Yemm and her bachelor brother, devoted churchwarden Mr. Benjamin Yemm.

A class from Lea School c.1910-1915
The man and woman on the left are probably Mr. and Mrs. Edkins. (Mrs. Edkins was
headmistress from 1909 to 1927.)
The lady on the right is Miss Elizabeth Watkins, assistant teacher for many years.
(HRO ref BA.38)

The appointment of Mrs. Edkins was unusual in that she had a husband and a daughter; most positions at that time were given to widows without dependants or to spinsters – that is, to ladies who were obliged to earn their own living. In 1913, Mrs. Edkins' daughter, Winifred, became a monitress in the school as Miss Watkins had done. Mr. James Edkins was a maker of clocks and watches and, somewhat unusually, appears to have been allowed to advertise and run his business from Lea School House. Mrs. Edkins remained at the school until 1927, again suggesting that, like her predecessor Mrs. King, she was not dissatisfied with her life in the village.

King George V was crowned in June 1911 amidst great pomp and splendour, and in November that year the king and queen travelled to India for an equally lavish coronation durbar in Delhi, essentially to emphasise their status as king-emperor and queen-empress and to demonstrate Britain's power in the world. Traditionally, celebratory gatherings such as these served to refresh and sustain political alliances and to strengthen family ties. The coronation in London, for example, was attended by the king's numerous cousins, some of whom travelled from Russia, Norway, Denmark, Greece, Mecklenburg, Bavaria, Hanover, Montenegro and Spain. Times were changing, however, and the old ties of kinship had become less assured and less dependable since Queen Victoria's death. Thus, when King George V declared war in August 1914, it was not solely on his aggressively militaristic cousin, Kaiser Wilhelm II of Germany, but on all of Britain's enemies and on behalf of the whole Empire. The government's notions of

The Revd. Buee in Lea Churchyard with workmen who were probably working on the
boundary wall at the time the churchyard was extended.
(By kind permission of Mrs. H. Edwards)

Empire would be tested to the full, and its role in providing manpower, food and other provisions would be crucial to Britain's survival. At home troops were mobilised, reservists and territorials were called to arms, and volunteers from all walks of life stepped forward to enlist for military service.

In rural parishes like the Lea the call to arms caused a serious labour shortage at one of the busiest times in the farming year, so, at the farmers' request, many adolescent boys were allowed to stay away from school to help bring in what promised to be an excellent harvest. The managers of some schools also gave permission for lessons to finish early so that teachers and children could spend part of the afternoon collecting nuts, wild fruits and horse-chestnuts. Blackberries, for example, were either preserved for use by the Armed Forces or used for jam making; horse-chestnuts were used in the manufacture of anti-gas masks. As the war lengthened and food shortages increased, schools were also encouraged to bring school gardens into food production. School log books reveal that boys, in particular, spent some lesson time gardening, and since there was quite a large garden attached to the school house, it is almost certain that Mrs. Edkins sanctioned similar arrangements at the Lea. On some occasions children were allowed to leave school half an hour earlier than usual in order to do 'National Service'. It is unclear just exactly what 'National Service' meant, though potato picking, pea picking and fruit picking spring to mind, but, bearing in mind that children could stay at village schools like the Lea until they reached working age at 14, it is quite probable that a group of well supervised boys and girls aged 13 and 14 could complete many of the tasks normally carried out by men who were then serving in the Armed Forces. Britain was fighting for survival.

Although everyone would have known that Britain was at war and that everyone, children included, had a duty to do whatever could be done to support the war effort, it is questionable just how much the general public would have known about the progress of events in Europe. In the absence of radio and television, the only source of information was the newspapers, but it is almost certain that some families would not have been able to read them adequately, even if they had had the means to buy them on a daily basis. It was perhaps with this in mind that the headmaster of one local school noted in his log book that he had allowed the children of standards V and VI, those aged 13 and 14, to read newspaper reports about government measures to stabilise food prices at home after a spate of panic buying, and also news of military successes in France and Belgium. Like many other headmasters and headmistresses in the district he would have been very much aware that some of his charges were worried about fathers or older brothers who had enlisted for military service, and this was probably a thoughtful attempt to allay their fears. Indeed, many thousands of brave young men left their villages to do service for their country, and in almost every parish church a memorial acknowledges that some of them never came home. The names of several young men, almost certainly taught by Mrs. King, Miss Watkins and Mrs. Edkins, are listed on the memorial in Lea Church.

In 1916, the government set up a Ministry of Reconstruction in readiness for the end of hostilities, and central to its aims was a major overhaul of education. The government had been forced to accept that the progress of the war had exposed many weaknesses in the British system and that improvement was urgently needed if Britain was to remain competitive with Europe. The result of the overhaul was the Education Act of 1918. This gave local authorities wider powers but the weakness of the Act was that many of its provisions were optional, which undermined any notion of a unified national system because some provisions were adopted in some areas but not in others. So, as the 1920s dawned, little had really changed. The children of the privileged classes continued to go to expensive fee-paying schools; the children of the masses continued to go to free day schools until they started work at 14. The grammar schools straddled the two systems and allowed for some social mobility, but in general, educational provision was still based on social class. Historian A.J.P. Taylor summed up the situation very neatly when he stated that: 'The two systems of education catered for different classes and provided education, different in quality and content, for rulers and ruled.'[1]

Chapter 6
War and Economic Depression

In 1918 Lea School was almost 60 years old. Hundreds of children had passed through its doors, but despite their lessons on the British Empire and the celebration of Empire Day with a church service and a half day holiday, few of them would have had any real experience or understanding of life beyond the village. The coming of the railways and the establishment of Mitcheldean Road Station no doubt aided communication with the wider world, but apart from the chance of an occasional Sunday School excursion to the seaside, their use lay beyond the means of most families. The school therefore remained a regular source of news, not least, about the progress of the war. Indeed, it was probably when the children gathered for morning assembly with Mrs. Edkins and Miss Watkins, sometimes joined by the Revd. Charles Buee, that important announcements were made, though none could have been more welcome than the news that the armistice had been signed and hostilities between England and Germany had ceased. This news would have been particularly poignant for some children because six men of the parish had lost their lives in the conflict although, owing to a distressing administrative mishap, only five names appear on the memorial in Lea Church. The First World War had shaken European civilisation as never before and had resulted in an incalculable loss of life. In towns and villages everywhere people were having to come to terms with the loss of husbands, fathers, uncles, brothers, sons and sweethearts – men who had fought and died in pursuit of a dynastic squabble.

Queen Victoria had long been referred to as the 'Grandmother of Europe' and the name was literally accurate, because eight of her nine children married into foreign royal families and as a result she had grandchildren of numerous nationalities. By a strange quirk of history, for many years this brought a social cohesion to the patchwork of European powers, but the hostilities of the years 1914-1918 damaged that unity to the point of destruction. By the end of the war the political map of Europe and Russia had been drastically altered and ruling dynasties had been severely weakened or completely swept away. Tsar Nicholas II of Russia, the Tsarina Alexandra, Queen Victoria's granddaughter, and their five children had been murdered and the royal family abolished. In Germany, Kaiser Wilhelm II, Queen Victoria's grandson, had been forced to abdicate and leave his plenipotentiaries to sign the armistice whilst he fled to seek sanctuary in Holland. In England, King George V, another grandson, ruled over a country greatly weakened by the many demands of war, and he also witnessed the first signs of the slow disintegration of the once all-powerful British Empire.

The 1918 Education Act had been a bold attempt to reform and expand the country's inadequate education system but as a result of post-war financial restraints, many of its clauses were soon modified, postponed or completely abandoned. In the aftermath of war, with the country in the grip of a major epidemic of influenza and an economic recession looming, the government had so many pressing problems that, at such a difficult time, education was not a major priority. The initial burst of economic activity which followed the armistice soon faded, not least in the coal mining areas. The government had taken direct control of coal production during the war, and it was not until 1921 that it returned control to private ownership. Unfortunately, this coincided with the arrival of reparation shipments of coal from Germany, and the home market collapsed. The mine owners' response was to burden their miners with longer working hours and to impose savage reductions in wages. These harsh and ill-considered measures merely resulted in strikes, unemployment and great social hardship, and many mining areas were in turmoil. Crucially for local people, the Forest of Dean mines were affected, which almost certainly had a negative impact on the nutrition and general well-being of some Lea families.

The 1920s were years of hardship, if not poverty, for most ordinary working people, and there were many privations to be endured, but life was not all doom and gloom

Miss Sybil Havergal of Castle End House with her Bible Group (1907)
(by kind permission of Mrs. H. Edwards)

because there were sporting diversions and village entertainments to be enjoyed. For many years, before and after the war, the Revd. Charles Buee was a constant source of support and encouragement for the village football team. Miss Sybil Havergal of Castle End House, the niece of hymn writer Frances Havergal, was an enthusiastic organiser and trainer of a group of handbell ringers; and the rectory room behind the church

The Revd. Buee with his wife and son
(by kind permission of Mrs. H. Edwards)

was the venue for choir suppers and regular church socials at which music for dancing was provided by Mrs. Edith Edwards at the piano and Mr. Harry Rudge playing the violin. These activities may seem rather quaint now but almost a century ago, before the arrival of recorded music, any small village community with musicians willing to play in public was fortunate indeed.

In 1923, after many years of loyal service to church, parish and school, the Revd. Charles Buee left the Lea to take up a living in Yorkshire and, after the customary three-month interregnum, he was followed by the Revd. Gilbert Ensor, M.A. of Merton College, Oxford. He soon became as familiar a figure at the school as his predecessors, visiting two or three times each week to assist with religious teaching and to oversee the preparation of the 14-year-old children for confirmation before they left school to begin work. Parishioners who were pupils in the early 1930s recall that he was a very musical person and that he did a great deal to encourage and train the church choir which, at that time, was comprised of 12 men, 14 ladies and 6 or 8 boys. In the 1920s and the early 1930s the church remained a strong influence in society, and for many regular attendance at early Communion, Matins and Evensong was the accepted pattern of each Sunday. Most Sunday trading was prohibited and almost everything was closed for the quiet observance of the Lord's Day.

In 1927, after 18 years as headmistress, Mrs. Edkins relinquished her post and she and her family appear to have left the area because their names fade from the records. The school log book indicates that her successor, Mrs. Emily Jane Carter, had been appointed in time for the beginning of the autumn term and that she was assisted by Miss Phyllis Yarnold, who taught the infants. Elderly parishioners recall that Mrs. Carter was a regular attender at church and that she was also an able organist. In her class teaching she was considered to be firm but fair, an excellent storyteller, and also she appears to be remembered with some affection.

Mrs. Carter's years as headmistress, 1927-1935, coincided with a period of enormous political, economic and social upheaval. The post-war depression and resultant austerity persisted, leading to widespread demonstrations, strikes against wage reductions, and hunger marches to London by those suffering the effects of enduring unemployment.

On a more positive note, British women finally achieved complete suffrage. Women over 30 had been given the vote in 1918, in recognition of their contribution to the war effort and in 1928 the law was changed to give them the vote at 21, the same as men. Many men and some women thought this both shocking and dangerous and no doubt they were still not reconciled to the election of the first female Member of Parliament when Viscountess Nancy Astor (1879-1964) took her seat in the House of Commons in 1919. Britain was changing, and that change was urgently needed.

The 1914-1918 war had exposed serious weaknesses in the education and general health of both conscripts and volunteers, so much so that in government circles there appeared to be an acceptance that in some respects Britain was falling behind other countries. In Europe there were ominous signs of the rise of Fascism, but when Adolf Hitler became Chancellor of Germany in January 1933, Churchill's warnings about future German aggression were mocked and went unheeded, and he was branded a warmonger. Britain, however, remained economically and militarily weak and soon, very soon, the loyalty of the men of the British Empire would be called on once more. Unfortunately, against this backdrop, there was little money available for vigorous educational reform, so schools had to do the best they could with the resources available to them.

In March 1927, when Mrs. Carter took up her post as headmistress, the buildings and facilities at Lea School had changed very little since the addition of an infant classroom in 1873. The average number of pupils at that time hovered between 60 and 70, all of whom were taught in the two original classrooms which were frequently very overcrowded. Despite these severe limitations, pupil attendance was excellent, and often

Lea School – probably taken in the 1920s

34

earned the children an additional half-day holiday. This says much about the happy atmosphere in the school and the teaching skills of Mrs. Carter and Miss Yarnold, a point not lost when the school was inspected in March 1928. After what appears to have been a very thorough inspection, His Majesty's Inspector, Mr. P.W. Scott, found no fault with the teachers, their teaching methods or the children's progress, but he did criticise the overcrowding in the infant room and suggested that the children who were sitting on sheets of brown paper on the floor should be provided with hessian or rush mats. This was an issue for the school governors, or managers, as they were then known, and largely beyond the control or the responsibility of the teachers.

At the end of September 1928, Miss Yarnold left and her place was filled by Miss Edith Carter, who was also an able organist. Shortly afterwards, mother and daughter were joined by Miss Kathleen Daniels, who transferred from Brockhampton School and assumed responsibility for teaching the infant class. Pupils from those days recall that from time to time they were also taught by Mr. Gordon Carter, Mrs. Carter's son, who was training for the priesthood and later secured a living in Devon. Essentially, though, the permanent teaching staff remained unchanged until Mrs. Carter's retirement in 1935.

Mrs. Emily Jane Carter (1870-1951), headmistress from 1927 to 1935, with her daughter, Miss Edith Carter (1902-1937), who taught at the school

In June, 1929 Mr. Scott made a return visit and, having scrutinised and signed the attendance registers, the admissions register, the school log book and the class timetables, went on his way, seemingly content with his findings. In December that year, Mr. F.M. Green, Assistant Diocesan Inspector, visited and seemed equally pleased, writing in the log book that: 'The Catechism has been carefully taught but there is room for further emphasis on the Sacramental principle. The answering on Holy Scripture was very good.'[1] He returned in July 1931 and wrote: 'This school continues to be very good and the older children give evidence of careful teaching when questioned on the Sacraments in which some weakness was apparent a year ago. Repetition was accurate and answering on Scriptural narratives was general and intelligent.'[2]

As the 1920s passed into the 1930s, the government appeared to be making a genuine effort to improve standards both in education and in children's health as far as possible within the limited resources available. Some Victorian notions remained firmly in place, but there was an attempt to broaden the range of curriculum activities, particularly for the older children. Miss Lawrence, for example, who had visited Lea School very regularly in her capacity as 'Needlework Inspectress', became 'Superintendent of Domestic Subjects', and in September 1930, Mrs. Carter wrote in the school log book that Miss Lawrence had made arrangements 'for 6 girls of 11+ to receive a 1st course of instruction in domestic subjects at the Ross Centre [Sir Walter Scott's School in Old Gloucester Road]. The girls to attend on Thursdays for a period of three terms.'[3] Later, Miss Mears, Physical Training Advisor, began calling and in December, 1934, Miss Perry, H.M.I. for Physical Training, visited and observed lessons in physical exercise taken in the playground and was clearly very pleased with what she saw. 'She greatly praised the manner in which teachers took their classes and the splendid efforts of the children performing the exercises of the New Syllabus prescribed by the Board of Education. She was also pleased that the teachers had attended the Course of Instruction provided by the L.E.A. at Ross.'[4] In addition to curriculum changes there was an attempt to broaden the children's horizons with summer outings arranged in conjunction with Lea Church Choir and the flourishing Sunday School. In July 1929 there was a trip to Burnham-on-Sea and in June 1933 a visit to Windsor.

Mrs. E.J. Carter cycling with her son, Mr. Gordon Carter, in around 1930

At the beginning of the 1914-1918 war there was considerable disquiet in military circles about the poor physical condition of many of the conscripts and volunteers who had presented themselves for medical examination, so much so that young men who were shown to be seriously undernourished were sent to special camps to gain weight before they were deemed fit enough to commence basic military training. The School Medical Service was an important means of monitoring child health and the health of the future workforce. In many households treatment was often neglected or delayed purely on the grounds of cost, because most visits to or from a doctor and most of the medicines prescribed had to be paid for by the family. The National Health Service was still some 20 years away. The regular visits from school doctors, nurses and dentists served, therefore, to alert District Medical Officers of Health of outbreaks of dangerous childhood diseases

Mrs. E.J. Carter, Lea Schoolhouse Porch

and sometimes resulted in individual schools being closed for two or three weeks at a time to halt the spread of measles, mumps, chicken pox, scarlet fever or whooping cough. In May 1928, for example, Mrs. Carter noted in the school log book that the Director of Education had ordered that all children suffering the first stages of whooping cough must be excluded and later the same day, 23rd May, Dr. Campbell visited and suggested that the school should be closed until after the Whitsun holiday and not opened again until 8th June, to prevent more children becoming infected.

Routine inspections of all the children every few weeks also allowed observant school nurses to keep a close eye on basic cleanliness, and in this respect Lea School children benefitted greatly from the attention of Nurse Powell. She appears to have been an extremely efficient nurse and over a period of some 20 years she established a sound working knowledge of the families who were likely to introduce problems such as ringworm, scabies, impetigo or head lice into the school. There were predictable cases of children being sent home because they had 'verminous heads', but records suggest that such families were very few at Lea School.

In the late 1920s and early 1930s low wages, unemployment and poverty made times difficult for many families, but ordinary people had few expectations and life drifted along at a predictable pace. Life was labour-intensive and the older children were expected to be helpful. Girls helped their mothers with domestic chores: boys looked after the chickens, filled the coal scuttle, brought in the logs and ensured that there was dry kindling wood for lighting the morning fire. Very few families in rural areas lived in dwellings wired for electricity and even fewer had ready access to a telephone.

In January 1935 Mrs. Carter recorded in the school log book that: 'Before schooltime this morning the caretaker came to the house to report damage done to the boundary wall and the boys' lavatories during the night by marauders. I reported the damage to the Correspondent who at once phoned to the Police Station. The Inspector of Police came out in the afternoon and is now carrying out investigations.'[5] The Correspondent was someone officially designated to handle correspondence and other communications between the School Managers, the Diocese and the County Board of Education. At that time the Revd. Gilbert Ensor was both Chairman of the Board of Managers and the official Correspondent and, fortunately, close at hand at the rectory just across the road from the school. Clearly, Mrs. Carter did not have the use of the telephone at the school or the school house or she would have telephoned the police herself. Mrs. Carter appears to have been a very efficient headmistress who presided over a well organised, benignly disciplined and essentially happy school. She resigned her post as headmistress at Easter 1935 and, with her husband and their daughter Edith, retired to live in Burnham-on-Sea in Somerset. However, Mrs. Carter's link with the school remains strong to the present day because her great granddaughter is a member of staff and three generations of her descendants still live in the village.

Chapter 7
Constitutional Crisis

Although the tragedies of the First World War were still raw for many families, the 1920s and the 1930s were patriotic times. Pupils from those years remember that the Union Jack always flew above the school on St. George's Day and again a month later for Empire Day, and that the school closed to mark royal occasions. In June 1934, for example, a day's holiday was granted when the Duke and Duchess of York, later King George VI and Queen Elizabeth, visited Hereford for the Three Counties Show and again in November that year when the Duke of Kent visited Mitcheldean. Royal visits were always important in maintaining loyalty to the monarchy and sustaining public morale, particularly when times were bleak. In 1934, great dangers were looming on the horizon as the threat of further German aggression had not gone away, but the gloom was lifted temporarily the following year when schools closed for several days at the beginning of May as part of the nation's celebration of King George V's Silver Jubilee. The jubilation was sadly soon dispelled. In 1936 a constitutional crisis of seismic proportions rocked the country and the Empire, just when public confidence was at a low ebb because war seemed ever more likely.

In January 1936, George V died and was succeeded by his eldest son, who ruled as King Edward VIII. He was unmarried but had formed an attachment with an American woman, Mrs. Wallis Warfield Simpson, who was divorced from her first husband and still married to her second, Ernest Simpson. She was therefore viewed as a manifestly unsuitable person to become a queen and an empress. In government circles and at Court everyone hoped that the king's infatuation with her would dwindle away as he became more heavily involved in his royal duties. George V and Queen Mary had strongly disapproved of their son's behaviour. The queen had promised the dying king that she would never receive Mrs. Simpson at Court, and despite her son's entreaties, she kept her promise. The infatuation did not diminish, and soon the king was faced with a painful dilemma. He could end his association with Mrs. Simpson and seek a more appropriate wife from amongst the British nobility or one of the royal houses of Europe, or he could abdicate and gamble everything on marrying Mrs. Simpson, when and if she managed to obtain a second divorce. He chose Mrs. Simpson. All sections of society were greatly shocked by his decision because in putting his own personal happiness first, he had abandoned his loyalty to his countrymen and his millions of subjects throughout the Empire. The abdication and rumours of the king's pro-German leanings shook the public's confidence in the monarchy. It seemed that loyalty was a very one-sided notion, particularly after all the sacrifices of the 1914-1918 war, and an air of despondency descended upon the population.

It was in the midst of this constitutional and political upheaval that Mrs. Carter's successor, Miss Gladys Davies, B.A., began to establish herself as one of Lea School's longest serving head teachers. Miss Davies had previously taught at Abenhall School and so, unlike some of her predecessors who had moved from places as far away as Somerset or Liverpool, she was not unfamiliar with the area. She also had relatives living at Lea; for example, Mrs. Edith Edwards, who sometimes played the organ for church services, was her cousin. It is quite possible that Miss Davies sometimes attended the church socials at which Mrs. Edwards played the piano for dancing in the Rectory Room. In rural areas, young unmarried ladies, schoolmistresses in particular, still had to be very careful about where they went and what they did, but dancing at a church social and in the company of a married female relative would no doubt have been readily approved by even the most vigilant parish censors. Miss Davies is well remembered for her precise organisation and very firm discipline. She was also greatly respected as an excellent teacher, and served the school as headmistress for 26 years.

Official inspection reports indicate that Mrs. Carter left the school in good heart and with a splendid attendance record, a record sustained by Miss Davies with the weekly average reaching between 92% and 96% for much of the time. This was no doubt helped by regular monthly visits from Attendance Officers for both Herefordshire and Gloucestershire Boards of Education who routinely took the names and addresses of children who were absent without explanation or apparent good cause. The weekly average rarely fell below 90% unless attendance was hampered by flu epidemics, outbreaks of childhood diseases such as measles, chicken pox and whooping cough, or spells of very severe weather – an enviable record, and one which often earned the children an extra half-day holiday.

In January 1937, when His Majesty's Inspector, Mr. F.W. Thompson, visited the school, the number of children on roll had fallen to 45, all of whom were taught by Miss Davies and the infant teacher, Miss Kathleen Daniels. Despite pointing out some weaknesses in the English and arithmetic of one group of children, he appears to have been quite favourably impressed with Miss Davies's organisation and attention to detail. He wrote in his report that: 'The present Head Mistress, who has not held the post of Head Teacher before, has prepared a new scheme of work and Time Table which appears to be working satisfactorily.'[1] Later he went on to say that: 'She takes a keen interest in her duties, she is trying to widen the children's outlook by means of broadcast talks and by the introduction of simple handwork, and she studies the welfare of those who remain at school for the midday meal.' The manifestation of dinner ladies and classroom assistants was still some way off in the future.

At that time, inspection reports were not published or made public. They remained confidential to the head teacher and the school managers, the county education authorities and, in the case of church aided schools, the diocesan inspectorate. Very few

This photograph of a classroom at the Elms boy's boarding school at Colwall Green shows, in the rows on the left, the type of backless desk commented on by Mr. F.W. Thompson in his inspection report for 1933. (Tim Ward collection)

head teachers, then as now, looked forward to inspections, but the reports produced were often successful in nudging, if not shaming, various education authorities into improving working conditions for both children and teachers. In 1928, for example, H.M.I. Mr. P.W. Scott, had drawn attention to the inappropriateness of children in the infant class sitting on sheets of brown paper on the floor[2] and in 1933, H.M.I. Mr. F.W. Thompson commented that: 'the desks of the older children are all of the long backless pattern'.[3] In 1937, the same inspector reported that: 'The children's comfort has been increased by the provision of new desks'.[4] Later in the same report he drew attention to the very unsatisfactory state of the playground, stating that: 'unfortunately the very poor playground surface is a serious handicap to teachers and children in Physical Training lessons'. 18 months later, in September 1938, Miss Davies noted in the school log book that a number of repairs had been carried out during the summer holidays, including improvements to the playground.

Although Lea parish is in Herefordshire and the school's general administration was the responsibility of the Herefordshire Board of Education, for ecclesiastical purposes at that time it was included in the rural deanery of The Forest (north) and the archdeaconry and diocese of Gloucester, and the Gloucester Diocesan Council of Education sent its inspectors to Lea School on an almost annual basis. In January 1936, Mr. D. Gethyn Jones visited the school and was clearly very pleased with his findings because he began his report by saying: 'It has been a real pleasure to inspect this school.'[5] He praised the teaching in both the infant and upper school classes and concluded his report with the compliment that: 'the general tone of the school is most commendable'. In March 1938 he returned and wrote in equally glowing terms of 'a very happy inspection of a school with an excellent tone'.[6]

It seems that Lea School was continuing to live up to its role as a church school, and in a manner that would have pleased and delighted its founder, the Revd. William David Hall. Mr. Gethyn Jones said of Miss Davies that: 'The Head Mistress has worked conscientiously and her careful teaching has given most gratifying results in practically the whole syllabus'. Of Miss Daniels he stated that: 'The infants are delightfully taught, and the various types of expression work shown, reveal carefully planned and well carried out teaching. The use of a very good new set of pictures is of immense value. These are skilfully used.' Mr. Gethyn Jones was ahead of his time in his thinking about infant teaching and infant teachers. There was, and still is to some extent, even in the 'enlightened' twenty-first century, a commonly held perception that the older the pupil, the better the teacher needs to be. But it is more accurate to say that the older the pupil, the more the teacher needs to know about the subject; and the younger the pupil, the more the teacher needs to know about the art of teaching. The inspector clearly recognised this skill in Miss Daniels, and even now her pupils, all advanced in years, remember her as an excellent teacher and a very pleasant person. There was praise too for the Revd. Gilbert Ensor. The report concluded with this fine compliment: 'The Incumbent, by his constant care and visiting, has helped the Head Mistress to create an atmosphere of reverence and Christian outlook, unfortunately not always found in our schools.'

Curiously, in addition to these inspections, the school log book records that between January 1937 and February 1939, three different school inspectors made a further six visits to the school for seemingly trivial reasons. This seems rather odd. Inspectors do not generally visit schools to check registers or inspect lavatories. It seems likely that another agenda was at work. This sequence of events was particularly strange because no explanation for these visits appeared in the log book, and the school had recently received very positive inspection reports from both government and diocesan inspectorates. In the context of the events of those years, however, the purpose of these mysterious visits becomes clear. Covert preparations were being made for the swift evacuation of children from heavily populated industrial areas, should German aggression once more turn into war, and Lea was an ideal place because, as a rural area with probably more animals per square mile than people, it was not worth bombing. The village also had its own small railway station and a very easy link with the Midlands.

In the light of these covert researches, it seems highly likely that, despite diplomatic manoeuvres intended to reassure the general public, in government circles there was already an acceptance that war with Germany was fairly certain, if not inevitable. Miss Davies had obviously been a party to the preparation of contingency plans, to ensure that if the need arose, they could slide smoothly into operation at very short notice. She was no doubt sworn to secrecy, which probably accounts for the brevity of her log book entries concerning visits from inspectors. She was in many ways the right person for Lea School at that time. She lived in the school house, could drive and had her own car. She was a strong, vigorous, mature young woman in her thirties, clear-thinking, shrewd and highly efficient. As political events in Germany began to gather momentum, those who had mocked Churchill's warnings about war were about to realise that his judgement would soon be proved correct and that very testing times lay ahead for everyone.

Chapter 8
Evacuees

In January 1933, when Field-Marshall Paul von Hindenburg, the President of the German Reich, appointed his new Chancellor, he did so with grave misgivings and considerable reluctance. The man in question was Adolf Hitler. Little by little, Hitler consolidated his influence and power until he had supreme control, and in August 1934, when Hindenburg died, he became a dictator and very quickly embarked on his expansionist plans. In March 1939, Bohemia and Moravia were annexed and declared a German Protectorate; Lithuania ceded Memel to Germany; and an anti-Polish propaganda campaign was mounted in the German press. This could mean only one thing: the necessity of convincing the German people of the justification of an intended invasion of Poland.

All Europe watched and waited. In April, the British Government introduced conscription into military service for all 18 year old males and in May an Anglo-Polish defence treaty was signed in London. German forces invaded Poland on 1 September 1939 and, since the British Government was committed to come to Poland's aid under the recently signed treaty, the mobilisation of the armed forces began on the same day. The following day compulsory military service was introduced for all men between 18 and 41 years of age, and a phased call-up programme began. Some men were exempt from call-up: those employed in munitions work, food production, mining and a few other trades and professions essential to the war effort. Britain's formal ultimatum to withdraw German troops from Polish soil was ignored and as a result war was declared on 3 September.

In the first four days of September, as a precaution against expected air raids, 1,200,000 people (mainly children) in England and Wales were moved from heavily populated industrial and urban areas to safer rural locations, and the many months of evacuation planning proved their worth. It is not clear from the school log book just when the first evacuees arrived at the Lea, but it is quite evident that Miss Davies was anticipating their arrival well before the formal declaration of war had been confirmed. The school opened for the autumn term on 28 August amidst an outbreak of measles amongst local children. The school was closed again on 1 September on the orders of the education authorities and Miss Davies noted: 'No lessons today owing to evacuation of school children to this district. The building to remain open but not for

Mitcheldean Road Station, where the evacuees arrived
(By kind permission of Mrs. H. Edwards)

lessons until further notice'.[1] Anecdotal evidence confirms that the evacuees, referred to by Miss Davies as the 'Birmingham' children were in fact from Kingstanding and probably arrived by train in the first few days of September.

Children were evacuated as classes and usually with their teacher. No doubt it was hoped that this arrangement would help to smooth the way for children being removed from their homes and transported many miles to a very different place. It must have seemed very strange for children from an industrial area to find themselves in the depths of the countryside. It may be presumed that, having arrived at Mitcheldean Road Station, the children and their teacher, Miss Harris, were greeted by a reception committee and then escorted along Mill Lane to the centre of the village, where it is known that the children were allocated to local families. The allocation process appears to have been a rather random exercise, with foster parents picking out the children they thought they would like to take. The children and their parents had no say in the matter at all. The parents would have put their children on a train and waved them off, but would have had no idea who would be looking after them or where they would be sleeping that night. It must have been very stressful for both parents and children.

Inevitably, some things went wrong. After the children had been chosen by or assigned to different local families and their names and addresses had been recorded, the various groups dispersed, but one small girl aged about 7 or 8 had apparently been overlooked and left behind. She was spotted by some young men working at the nearby garage, and they kept a watchful eye on her . When it seemed clear that no one was going to come back for her, they became increasingly concerned for her safety. Fortunately, the little girl herself did not appear to be anxious or distressed, but merely waited patiently with her small suitcase. After some debate with his workmates, one of the young men, much to his credit, decided to take her to his mother for safety when he went home to lunch. Through his intervention the story had a happy ending because the child became a playmate for his younger sister and stayed with the family for the duration of the war. Although she has now lived far away for many years, she continues to be in regular contact with her old foster family. It could, however, have ended very differently but for the young man's very adult sense of responsibility, and the incident shows how vulnerable evacuated children could be.

Some children, however, were evacuated in more secure circumstances because they were evacuated with their parents. Ray Bilby, for example, was evacuated to the Lea from the London area as a result of his father's work. The family lived at Lea Hall and he attended Lea School and remembers his time there as a largely happy experience. Whilst in Miss Davies's class he won a scholarship to Ross Grammar School and, having married a Ross girl, has remained in the area ever since. Lea parishioners who remember those days seem to think that the evacuees were generally well treated, but there is anecdotal evidence to suggest that a few took sudden and unexpected dips in the village pond – but then children will be children.

The school reopened on 11 September but only for the 'Birmingham' children; it remained closed to the local children pending authority from the Medical Officer of Health. In the days that followed Nurse Powell examined all the evacuated children, and authority to open the school for all children finally became operative from 25 September. Initially the children were taught in their separate classes with their own teachers, the local children from 8.45am until 12.45pm, and the evacuees for one long session in the afternoons. The gradual integration of the evacuees appears to have gone well, despite some accommodation difficulties, because in mid-October Miss Davies recorded that: 'the 'Birmingham' children are under the charge of Miss Harris who takes all the upper children for music three times a week during which time I assist with the infants. Three infant evacuees are working with the local infants. Otherwise lessons are separate'.[2] The days were becoming more like normal school routines in that the regular school sessions were by then from 9.30am to 12.30pm and 1.30pm to 3.30pm for all the children. It remains unclear how Miss Davies managed to accommodate all the children in two rooms, but it is evident that on some occasions the use of the Rectory Room near the church was of vital importance.

In late October 1939, the school dentist spent two days in school attending specifically to the needs of the evacuees and, since the infant room was needed as a surgery, Miss Daniels took the girls and younger boys for nature walks and then to the Rectory Room for lessons, including percussion and country dancing. In good weather, the older boys, those between 12 and 14 years of age, were sometimes employed in working on a part of the rectory garden which the Revd. Gilbert Ensor had allowed them to use as a school garden. This must have been a time of great adjustment for all the children. The evacuees had to get used to the countryside and a very different way of life away from their families; and the local children had to adjust to the fact that their school now included children who spoke with markedly different accents from their own. Also, some of their fathers were now away from home doing compulsory military service.

The routines of daily life did begin to settle down but nevertheless remained fluid. Voluntary evacuees – that is, children sent by their parents to stay with relatives or friends living in the countryside – sometimes arrived in twos and threes. School inspectors called occasionally to check seating accommodation, presumably to ascertain whether the school could take more children, whilst Police Constable Williams called to enquire into the behaviour of certain unnamed children. At the beginning of December Miss Harris, who had had charge of the evacuated children, returned to Birmingham, and all the children were merged into their respective age groups as one school.

The number of children on the roll at this time appears to have ranged between 40 and 60, with apparently quite frequent admissions, departures and re-admissions.

The Revd. Gilbert Ensor (Rector 1923-1940)
(By kind permission of Mrs. H. Edwards)

RA ROBERTSON, FEB 1989

Attendance was also affected by illness and the severity of the weather. The first winter of the war was harsh and even in early December 1939, Miss Davies recorded that: 'This week has been very cold and wet. One foster mother did not send evacuees to school owing to the inadequacy of [their] clothing'.[3] This was a common problem, compounded by the fact that the evacuated children remained the responsibility of their own local authority, so that host local authorities were not provided with funds to meet the deficiency. A myriad of clerks attempted to keep control of costs and the exchange of funds.

School attendance was disrupted throughout January 1940 and into February as a result of heavy falls of snow and intense frosts. It was impossible for many children to get to school, and even the few sturdy souls living nearby who did arrive for lessons had to be sent home again because the building was so cold that the ink pots were frozen solid. In addition, frozen pipes meant that there was no water, the toilets across the yard were completely beyond use and, of course, it was almost impossible to find a plumber because so many had been called up for compulsory military service. By the middle of February the weather had improved, but soon after the school reopened some children had to be excluded in order to contain an outbreak of German Measles. By the middle of March it was snowing hard again and no doubt everyone was relieved when the school closed once more, but this time for the much needed Easter holidays.

At the beginning of the summer term the weather improved greatly, providing everyone with some much needed warm sunshine; nature walks and physical training lessons were resumed and the older boys were again given the opportunity to work in the school garden, which had been abandoned during the harsh winter and cold, wet spring. Circumstances were, however, challenging and changing all the time, and Miss Davies presided over a fluid situation which required flexibility of thinking and regular amendment of plans. Evacuees continued to come and go, and some children had to be found new places because their foster parents had moved away or had to accommodate displaced or sick relatives from other parts of the country. At the end of April Miss Davies's trusted and reliable infant teacher, Miss Daniels, resigned from her post and was followed by a number of temporary teachers until a permanent appointment was made almost ten months later.

The school closed on 10 May for the Whitsun holiday, but the children were warned that they might be called back earlier by a message which would be broadcast on the radio if German forces entered Holland or Belgium. In the event, Holland, Belgium and Luxembourg were invaded and school reopened four days later. There then followed a rather confused situation regarding children working on the land during the wartime labour shortage. The local education authority appeared to approve the release of several of the older boys from lessons for this purpose, only to revoke the permission a week or two later. Finally, matters were resolved when the summer holidays were advanced by a week so that the children could assist with the haymaking and with pea-picking.

The ebb and flow of evacuees continued, particularly when the government stopped paying the full cost of foster care. As soon as parents were required to contribute to the costs, many of the children were taken back to their town and city homes to take their chances with everyone else. The rural working class housed the urban working class but some of the upper classes managed to avoid any direct contact with evacuees. They were, however, also having to make adjustments to the wartime situation because the depressed state of the economy and the poor state of the stock market meant that many had much reduced incomes. In addition, as more and more men were called to arms and their places in many walks of life were filled by women, the upper classes were greatly inconvenienced by the tiresome and vexing problem of engaging and retaining the services of reliable house servants.

Chapter 9
War Again

As the war gathered pace its effects began to impinge on almost every aspect of life. Food rationing was introduced to ensure that, as far as possible, everyone got a fair share of essential food items, and to that end every family had to be registered with a specified grocer and butcher who assiduously removed coupons from ration books as purchases were made each week. Once the week's allowance had been used no further purchases could be made until the following week. Later, the purchase of clothing was also rationed, but this was more difficult to control because less well off families frequently did not have the funds to use their allowances in full. They soon found other means of benefitting from them, however. The affluent, for whom money was not a problem, were quite prepared, if not eager, to pass on good quality clothes they no long wanted in exchange for clothing coupons other families could not afford to use. This was quite illegal, but it served its purpose. No doubt most officials were well aware of the situation and some almost certainly participated in such transactions themselves.

In towns, cities and villages everywhere mile upon mile of ornamental iron railings were removed to provide raw materials for the war effort, and in that regard Lea was no exception. Ross and Whitchurch Rural District Council wrote to the Parochial Church Council stating that: 'They had scheduled certain ornamental fences in the graveyard ...'[1] Scheduled meant, in effect, that the listed items were going to be requisitioned and there was not very much anyone could do about it. After some discussion the clerk to the PCC was instructed to write to the District Council stating that they had no objection to the removal of the fences 'provided that any damage done in the process should be made good'.[2]

In addition, numerous public, private and commercial buildings were inspected and, if deemed appropriate, were commandeered for government use: factories with suitable machinery were adapted for the production of military necessities; wards in former workhouses were cleared to provide accommodation for workers in munitions factories; and thousands of young men between 18 and 25 years old were directed to work in the mines to boost coal production instead of doing military service. In rural areas, large country houses were often requisitioned for use as government training centres, psychiatric hospitals or convalescent homes for military casualties, whilst their owners found themselves living in one of their own estate cottages.

Farmers were exhorted to bring additional land under cultivation in order to provide more food and, to aid them in this endeavour, over 90,000 young women from all social classes and walks of life enlisted in the Women's Land Army to fill the labour gap left by men called up for military service. Householders were encouraged to dig up lawns and plant every available space in their gardens with vegetables and, wherever possible, to keep chickens and a few pigs. If three or four pigs were kept and fattened for domestic use, however, at the time of slaughter half had to be sold to the government to help with the national food shortage. It was not uncommon, therefore, for one or two pigs to go for a little holiday when government food inspectors were around, only to return with a friend or two a few days later when the inspectors had moved on to another area. At that time many houses had a bacon rack suspended from the kitchen ceiling or in an outhouse and good housewives made use of every scrap of bacon they had. Britain was fighting for survival once more and nothing could be wasted.

It was against this backdrop, at the end of May 1940, that Miss Davies lost two of her greatest supporters. Miss Daniels left to become Mrs. Dunn, and the Revd. Gilbert Ensor gave up his living to retire. After 16 years of dedicated service to parish and school, the Revd. Ensor was greatly missed. The first baby he christened when he began his ministry in the village in 1924, a lifelong member of Lea Church, remembers him as a clever, kindly man, genuinely dedicated to his calling and a true guardian of the flock. He also followed in the footsteps of the Revd. Charles Buee in giving generously of his time to support the school as rector, teacher, Chairman of the Board of Managers and Official Correspondent.

His comments in the school log book when he called to check and sign the class attendance registers indicate that he had great confidence in Miss Davies as headmistress and held her in high regard. In April 1939, for example, when Miss Daniels was away on sick leave, he wrote: 'I called at 3.15 and checked the registers. Miss Davies is carrying on under the difficulty of being single handed – and doing so ably, but it is to be wished that assistance may soon be forthcoming.'[3] Just before Christmas 1939 he wrote: 'I called at 2.30pm and checked the registers. There was a good attendance, especially considering the severe weather, and everything was in good order.'[4] He also called on his last day at Lea but modestly made no mention of himself. 'I called at 2.30pm and checked the registers. There was a good attendance and all seemed to be going on as usual.'[5] He was saying that despite all the current difficulties, the school was in good hands.

It is customary for there to be a three-month interregnum between one parson leaving and another arriving, but it was not until February 1941, almost eight months after the Revd Ensor's departure, that Miss Davies noted briefly in the school log book that: 'The new rector of the parish visited the school this morning.'[6] He was the Revd E.C.A. Graham-Harrison, and records suggest that his participation in the life of Lea School was far less than that of his predecessors. He signed the school log book to confirm his checking of the attendance registers just twelve times between 3 February 1941 and 24 September 1943, but it is possible, of course, that during the war he had additional duties elsewhere which placed heavy limits on the time he could devote to the school. There is no mention of him at all from September 1943 until July 1946 but there is anecdotal evidence that during that time he was doing military service, presumably as a chaplain. After the war he appears to have moved on to another parish. The religious teaching in the school must, therefore, have been in Miss Davies's hands for much of the war period and, judging from diocesan inspection reports, she continued to do it very well.

In July 1941, Mr. G.W. Parker, Gloucester Diocesan Inspector, visited the school and wrote a very favourable report. He was pleased that most of the children were very responsive to his questions and that their answers were intelligent. He was also impressed by how well they knew and understood the catechism. The only criticism he could make was that some of the children spoke too quickly and, as a result, expression was lost. Despite this, he was pleased to say that the tone of the school was good and that 'Most satisfactory work is being done in this school'.[7] He went on to say: 'It cannot be easy as the ages, especially in the top class, vary a great deal and so the result is all the more creditable to the teachers.'[8]

A year later the school was inspected by Assistant Diocesan Inspector Mr. D.R.J. Mack, who wrote glowingly about the reverence of the morning prayers and hymn singing and the Bible knowledge of all age groups. He concluded his report by saying: 'There is ample evidence that the religious instruction throughout the school is sound and systematic, and presented in such a manner as to endeavour to interest the children.'[9] This was evidence, too, that Miss Davies and her staff did not merely give religious instruction by rote.

It says much for Miss Davies's organisation and planning that she managed to achieve so much, despite the difficult and ever-changing circumstances in which she – and her many contemporaries throughout the land – endeavoured to teach. In addition to the comings and goings of evacuees, and routine visits from the school doctor, nurse and dentist, there were unexpected closures resulting from epidemics of childhood diseases and the need for child labour in the fields, as well as staff illness and the shortage of supply teachers to replace them. In September 1942, for example, the school was closed for one month's 'holiday' for the children to help with potato lifting. On the day the school reopened, Miss Davies was given sick leave but, since no replacement could be found for her, she remained at her post. The following day, Nurse Powell made a routine visit to the school and, observing Miss Davies, urged her to go home. Two days later she was in hospital. A Mrs. Mary Sheila Thomas was put in charge of the school until Miss Davies returned to duty in late November.

The new year of 1943 brought snow, followed by a period of cold wet weather and, almost inevitably, children's absences through seasonal illnesses. By the middle of March, however, the weather had improved and outdoor activities were once again possible. In the school log book Miss Davies noted: 'I took the older children for a nature walk this afternoon. During the walk we picked violets and primroses to make a wreath for the funeral of Mr. Francis Wintle, for many years a manager of this school and a good friend to the children.'[10] He was indeed a good friend. Pupils of that time remember that he provided books, footballs and other games equipment for the school and that, at his own expense, each year he took two coachloads of children to see a pantomime at the theatre in Cheltenham and gave them tea in a restaurant before the journey home. This really was a treat to brighten the lives of children who rarely went anywhere, particularly during the privations of the war years.

Although every effort seems to have been made to keep life in school as normal as possible, reminders of war were ever-present in daily routines, even in a small rural parish. Each morning the children carried their gas masks to school and their teachers drilled them in the procedures for their correct use and how to put them on quickly should the need arise. Sergeant Little, the local Air Raid Precaution Officer, called regularly to check the masks, and teachers ensured that none were left behind in school when the children went home. The older children continued to be released from lessons for days and sometimes weeks to do potato picking or to get in the apple harvest, and there can be little doubt that they all saw military convoys pass the school on their way to Gloucester or, in the other direction, to Ross and Hereford. Mercifully, however, they would have known nothing of the air raids experienced by some of those evacuees who were quickly collected and taken home as soon as the government required parents to contribute to their children's maintenance in the countryside.

Despite all the interruptions to her teaching plans, Miss Davies appears to have succeeded, for the most part, in maintaining her own very high standards. She also managed to make time for the children to participate fully in the war effort, including village fund raising activities. In May 1943 she noted in the school log book that: 'Owing to "Wings for Victory" week, lessons have been rather disorganised this week. Children were taken to the Rectory Room three times to rehearse for an entertainment tonight.'[11] Miss Davies clearly worked very hard and expected the children to work hard too, but at the same time she appears to have been well aware that the children of those years were in danger of losing their childhood in the turmoil of war.

The annual diocesan inspections of religious education continued throughout the war years, and the reports were generally very good. Any slight weakness was explained by reference to events beyond Miss Davies's control and quickly absolved. In October 1943, for example, Assistant Diocesan Inspector, Mr. D.R.J. Mack, remarked that the older children were not quite up to the standard of the previous year – hardly surprising with so much time spent potato picking – but fully accepted that there were mitigating circumstances. He stated that at the time of the inspection: 'Nearly a third of the children were absent owing to epidemics, this and the absence during the past year – through illness – of the Head Teacher must have meant a serious set back to the work in this school ...'[12] but he concluded that 'there is every evidence that the Religious teaching is given with care and earnestness.'[13] In June 1944, the same inspector gave a very positive report and was clearly delighted with the bright, happy and responsive children he encountered in the infant room. He also acknowledged the difficulties presented by the comings and goings of children from other areas when he remarked that: 'This school includes quite a number of very recent arrivals from the evacuated areas whose religious education up to their entry has evidently been scanty, and who therefore could not be expected to answer. This recent influx must add to the difficulty of teaching children of varying ages and varying capacity.'[14] Surprisingly, in the midst of these complications, whilst the country was still at war, the government passed legislation which was to abolish the notion of the elementary school and replace it with primary and secondary schools. This was the Butler Act of 1944.

Chapter 10
Peace and Post-War Austerity

The mass recruitment of young men into the armed forces during the 1914-1918 war had made military commanders acutely aware of the nation's low educational standards, and after the war there remained in government circles a concern that England was falling behind other European countries. The fiscal restraints of the post-war economy prevented much real progress in educational reform, but the inadequate nature of the education provided for adolescents, in particular, was recognised as a problem which needed urgent action. A consultative committee, established under the leadership of Sir W.H. Hadow, was asked to review provision, and their report, 'The Education of the Adolescent', appeared in 1926. It concluded that the accepted description of schools as 'elementary' was confusing and recommended that it should be replaced by the terms 'primary' and 'secondary' education. In 1936, an Act was passed raising the school leaving age to 15 with effect from 1 September 1939, but its implementation was halted with the declaration of war just two days later. When the Butler Act was passed in 1944, it brought about a major overhaul of state education, but its provisions could only be introduced in phases because of wartime restrictions on finance. Meanwhile, life in schools continued much as before, and teachers struggled to make the best use of the buildings and meagre resources available to them.

The inadequacy of school buildings caused many problems, not least when school meals were introduced. At that time very few, if any, primary schools had any space which might be converted to a permanent kitchen or even enough room to provide a temporary one. School meals were therefore cooked at a central kitchen in Ross in buildings which stood on the site now occupied by Morrisons petrol filling station, and were then delivered to numerous local schools. In November 1943, a meeting of the school managers and representatives of the L.E.A. took place at Lea School to consider the practicalities of the venture, and no doubt those involved quickly came to the conclusion that the school buildings were too cramped for serving meals and another alternative would have to be found. The only appropriate building close enough to the school was the Rectory Room behind the church, and even this was not ideal, as using it meant taking the children out of school and across the busy Gloucester road twice a day and in all winds and weathers; the footpath which runs beside the churchyard wall was not constructed until December 1950 or January 1951.

January 1945 brought heavy snow and severe frosts. Miss Davies noted that the temperature in her classroom had not exceeded 40 degrees Fahrenheit for a week and, since the weather did not show any sign of improvement, after discussions with the school's Official Correspondent, it was decided to close the school. When it reopened a few days later, the classroom temperature at 9.30am was a mere 26 degrees and since more snow followed, the four hardy souls who arrived for lessons were sent home. The next day 11 pupils made an appearance but on the advice of the Director of Education, the school was closed for a further five days. After the extreme cold there followed the almost inevitable epidemics of measles and whooping cough and, of course, a further disruption of lessons.

In May, there was a much more welcome closure – a two-day holiday to celebrate the surrender of the German armed forces. There was great rejoicing and some four million servicemen began their journey home, but home to a much altered and exhausted land. In December two days, described as 'V.J.' holidays, were added to the Christmas break to celebrate the Japanese surrender. The war was finally over, but the austerity of the post-war years must have made many wonder why they had fought a war. They were the victors but, with the return of so many more people to feed, food rationing became even more stringent as bread and potatoes were added to the list, and the enormous task of rebuilding the country and repairing a shattered society still lay ahead.

Ever mindful of all the privations everyone had endured, Miss Davies clearly took every opportunity possible to lighten the children's days with frequent visits to places of interest. Not all age groups went on every visit, and it remains unclear how she managed to finance trips requiring transport, but manage she did, despite the austerity of the times. There was a walk to Bailey Wood to view a large swathe of foxgloves which had erupted

School photograph 1945-1946, Miss G. Davies Headmistress
(School Collection)

54

from long-dormant seeds after tree-felling and another to the village railway station where the station master explained how the signalling system worked. On another occasion, the children were taken to the site of a Roman town at a farm at Bromsash and later to Linton School, where the headmaster had arranged to show them some of the excavated relics. There was a visit to Flaxley Abbey and at the end of January 1946 the school was closed for the day for everyone to go to see a pantomime. It is quite evident that Miss Davies endeavoured to take the children out into the world as far as means allowed and also to bring the world into the school, not least through the means of the radio. Despite everything that had happened these were patriotic days. Arrangements were made for the children to listen to a special BBC radio broadcast on 24 May, to celebrate Empire Day, also Queen Victoria's birthday, and in June they listened to the King's Victory Day Message, just before breaking up for the Whitsun holidays.

By that time Lea School was beginning to return to its pre-war normality. The comings and goings of evacuees had ceased, classrooms were no longer uncomfortably crowded, gas masks were left at home, and during the autumn the school was completely redecorated. Mr. Charles Vale, a peripatetic music teacher, began to make regular visits to supervise singing and percussion lessons, and later helped the children to prepare for their carol concert.

In the weeks before Christmas 1946 the weather was wet and cold, and the first week of January brought ice and flurries of snow which proved to be the heralds of one of the worst winters on record. The first significant amount of snow fell on 24 January, and this was followed by more heavy falls over the next few days. Never one to waste words, at the end of the month Miss Davies wrote: 'Conditions worse – no cleaner – no fires. One lit by me and hot milk given to children present (11/45) then sent home about 10 a.m. Present temperature (10.25) 24 F.[1] The heavy snowfalls and hard frosts continued and on 10 February she wrote: 'After a heavy fall of snow over the weekend the lavatories were blocked by drifts. Nine children arrived but, as there were signs of a thaw it was decided to close till Thursday (12th) in the hope that the snow would have melted away and water be available for flushing lavatories etc.'[2] The thaw did not come and three days later she wrote: 'Similar conditions. 14/45. Only twice during the past three weeks has the thermometer registered more

The Church of St. John the Baptist, Lea, taken from the school garden

55

than 40 F. Less than 50F then'.[3] These conditions persisted throughout February and early in March she noted: 'After a blizzard which raged all night and is still continuing, it is impossible for the children to get to school.'[4] The next day she added: 'More snow during the night completely blocked the entrance to the school for scores of cubic yards. Hundreds of tons of snow are in the playground and lavatories are blocked. No wheeled traffic of any kind before midday. No buses afterwards nor little of any kind.'[5] The blizzards and very icy conditions persisted and not until 21 March was Miss Davies able to write: 'This week has been much milder, though very wet. av. att. 40/45'.[6] The warmer weather was no doubt a welcome relief after so many weeks of cold, icy conditions but unfortunately, as the thaw advanced, further disruption was caused by extensive flooding. One week later the school closed for the Easter holidays.

The reforms enshrined in the 1944 Education Act continued, but their implementation appears to have been rather patchy because of the inadequate nature of available buildings. In 1944, most children still remained in elementary schools until they were 14 years old and were able to seek employment. Those who went to grammar schools either gained entry because their parents could pay the necessary termly fees, or because they had won a scholarship and had their fees paid for them. In Ross, for example, children either went to the grammar school in Ryefield Road or remained in the elementary Board School in Cantilupe Road, which was located on the land now occupied by the public library and a small housing complex. The Butler Act of 1944 introduced the 11+ examination and abolished grammar school fees. The existing fee-paying pupils were allowed to stay until they had finished their education, but all new admissions were strictly on merit.

In the early 1950s a large new secondary modern school was built in Ross, just off Ledbury Road, for all children, including those from outlying parishes such as the Lea, who had not passed the 11+ examination. Later, with the advent of comprehensive education, the grammar school was closed and all children above the age of 11 went to the former secondary school, renamed as John Kyrle High School. The school in Cantilupe Road became a primary school for children of 5 to 11 years and was later renamed as Ashfield Park Primary School when it moved to its present location. The old grammar school became the Ryefield Centre and its later extension became the Larraperz Centre. But in 1947 all of this was still in the future, and with the raising of the school-leaving age to 15 in April 1947, there appeared to be an inadequate number of places for the older children. The new secondary modern school was still some years away and so provision had to be found for them wherever space was available. In September that year Miss Davies recorded, with more than a hint of exasperation, that: 'Senior children who expected to attend Weston-under-Penyard School on 23rd Sept: have been recalled to this school pending completion of preparations at Weston'.[7] It was not until 1 December 1947 that they finally began attending school at Weston. Arrangements for Lea children post 11 years of age remained the same until the new secondary school was opened in Ross in the early 1950s.

The world into which these youngsters had been born in the early 1930s had changed enormously even during their lifetime and so had Britain's status as the ruler of a vast

Drawing of Lea School by R.A. Robertson

Empire. In their geography lessons Miss Davies had no doubt taught them that all the countries shaded pink on the map of the world were part of the British Empire, but before they were grandparents that Empire would be no more. In August 1947, for example, after partition on religious lines, India and Pakistan were granted independence. The 'Jewel in the Crown' had gone and, after King George VI and Queen Elizabeth, there would be no more king-emperors or queen-empresses. There were, however, still school holidays to mark royal occasions. In November 1947, the school closed for a day to celebrate the marriage of H.R.H. Princess Elizabeth to Philip Mountbatten, Duke of Edinburgh, and in April 1948, a two day holiday was granted to celebrate the Silver Wedding of King George and Queen Elizabeth.

By this time the number of children on the roll appears to have fluctuated between 35 and 50, and after the departure of the 11-15 year olds, the school began to settle into its new form as a primary school. The diocesan inspector's report for that year, however, illustrated just how far the thinking of managers needed to change before primary schools would really reflect their name in essence and organisation. In October 1948 the inspector wrote: 'I enjoyed my visit to this village school, where the work goes on quietly and conscientiously. The children responded well to questions. It was good to find the Prayer Book used in Opening Worship. It would certainly help if the Managers could supply a piano, as a harmonium is not the best of instruments for use in a school.'[8] The use of a harmonium to accompany children of 12 or 14 might just have been acceptable, but for infants and juniors it was totally inappropriate. It was not until July 1949 that a new piano arrived in the school but, to their credit, the school managers had taken the point. They were having to adjust to the fact that a primary school was not just a trimmed elementary school, but something quite different. To meet the needs of 5- to 11-year-olds required new thinking, a fresh approach and time to evolve. Lea School, like many others, needed new buildings too, but they would be a long time coming. In the post-war years there were more pressing priorities: the rebuilding of large areas destroyed by bombing; the urgent need to increase the housing stock; and the fulfilment of the promise to improve the nation's health care provision. In the past, families had avoided or delayed seeking medical advice because of the cost but now, with the introduction of the National Health Service in July 1948, anyone could see a doctor and seek proper treatment without having to worry about how to pay for it.

Chapter 11
The New Elizabethan Age

In October 1913, Mrs. Edkins wrote in the admission register that Mr. John Bowes of Lea Post Office had withdrawn his three sons Louis, Hector and Eric from school. The reason given for their departure was simply 'Gone to Australia'. Ever since the last decades of Queen Victoria's reign, the 1880s and the 1890s, British politicians had encouraged emigration to the far corners of the British Empire in order to populate it with people who would spread British values and influence throughout the world and, at the same time, retain a natural allegiance to the mother country. That wise Victorian thinking had proved its worth, because the men of the Empire had answered loyally the call to arms to defend Britain in two world wars, but by 1946 she could no longer afford all her commitments to the Empire, and it was time to rethink policy.

Miss Davies (1907-1998), like the Bowes children, had been born into an increasingly unstable Edwardian world and into a generation brought up to be proud of the British Empire and to understand its vital importance to Britain's future security. It can only be surmised, therefore, what thoughts passed through her mind when, in May 1946, she noted in her log book that the school would close to celebrate Empire Day, well aware that it was almost certainly for the last time. Although she remained at the school until 1961, Empire Day was not mentioned again. India was granted independence in 1947, and within 30 years the Empire it had taken two centuries to build had been completely dismantled.

At the end of January 1952, Princess Elizabeth and the Duke of Edinburgh embarked on a royal tour to Australia and New Zealand to acknowledge the support those countries had given and the sacrifices their people had made during the last war. On 6 February, however, the king died and the princess returned to England as Queen Elizabeth. In towns and cities throughout the kingdom people paused to listen to the proclamation of the queen's succession to the throne. In Ross, the children from the school in Cantilupe Road were taken along Gloucester Road to the corner of Broad Street to listen to the town crier read the proclamation from the market house steps; and at Lea School, the children were given a treat for this special occasion. Miss Davies recorded that: 'At 10.50am I took the children of my class into my house to see by television the proclamation of Her Majesty Queen Elizabeth at St. James' Palace and Temple Bar.'[1] Since very few families owned televisions at that time, this was a memorable event.

By the early 1950s, the social fabric of Britain had changed for ever and it was clear that ordinary members of the general public were in some ways less respectful towards authority, less deferential towards the upper classes, and less traditional in their notions of England's status in the world. In the years from 1946 to 1949 over a million young men and women emigrated from Britain to Australia, New Zealand and Canada but curiously, this generation was not dismayed or even greatly concerned about the loss of Empire. England was exhausted and they saw Australia, New Zealand and Canada as young, largely English speaking countries, offering opportunities for a fresh start and the chance of a better life. Some people viewed the Commonwealth as a poor substitute for the Empire, but King George VI had always sustained an unshakeable belief in it and, under the quietly resolute guidance of his daughter, the present Queen Elizabeth II, the Commonwealth of Nations has flourished and grown continuously in both power and influence in the world.

In 1952, Britain was still coming to terms with the aftermath of war. Many everyday things were still on ration, not least sweets and chocolate, because of the shortage of sugar. It is now almost unimaginable to most children that previous generations could not just buy sweets whenever they liked. The family ration book had to be produced and inspected by the shopkeeper, who removed the coupons necessary for each and every purchase. Once the week's allocation had been used, no more purchases could be made until the following week, and no shopkeeper could afford to be casual or careless about regulations for fear of having to face very uncomfortable questions from the local administrators who monitored food rationing. Sweets and chocolate were removed from rationing just in time for the celebration of the queen's coronation, 2 June 1953.

Lea School closed for the Whitsun and Coronation holidays on 22 May, and just before the children went home, the Rev. H.L. Whatley talked to the older children about the meaning and significance of the coronation as a religious service and then presented all the children with commemorative spoons provided by Herefordshire County Council. The coronation brought a morale-boosting splash of colour to an otherwise grey and gloomy land and, despite all the shortages, street parties were held everywhere. The country had a new, young queen and fresh optimism for the future and, hopefully, a second golden Elizabethan Age.

At Easter 1953, the faltering implementation of the Butler Act of 1944 took a decided step forward in the Ross area with the opening of the new secondary modern school at Overross. Its space and facilities widened the scope of adolescent education, and at the same time, it eased overcrowding in many village schools just in time for them to accommodate the post-war baby boom. At the beginning of the autumn term in September 1950, Lea School, for example, had just 31 children on the roll. They ranged in age from 5 to 13 years, with the 13+ children still attending a class at Weston-under-Penyard School. The numbers were, however, predicted to rise in the near future, and there were growing concerns about the lack of classroom space and the complete absence of washing facilities in the boys' cloakroom. In addition, there was still no artificial light in the school buildings, and it remained unclear when electricity would become available. The lack of electricity was not quite as unusual as younger generations might think, because at that time many rural homes were still lit by oil lamps or candles.

In May 1954, Miss Davies noted that she had admitted two more children from the new houses at Knightshill and that with their arrival the school was now overcrowded and she had been advised not to admit any more. Although the building of new houses at Knightshill caused some accommodation problems for a while, it did bring other benefits. The electricity supply had to be extended, and it was at about this time that the school buildings were wired for electric light for the first time. By June 1954, the number of children on the roll had risen to 56, and as a result it became clear that the children's washing facilities were now totally inadequate for the number of children using them. Miss Davies does not appear to have allowed these issues to trouble her too greatly because, of course, they were largely beyond her control. The H.M.I. reports of her management and teaching were generally very good and the diocesan reports excellent, so, having survived an overcrowded school during the war years, she appears to have taken the limitations of the buildings, and all the daily complications they created, completely in her stride.

When parents complained that condensation on the walls of the girls' cloakroom made their coats wet, Miss Davies simply summoned a member of the County Architect's Department to assess the situation and suggest possible solutions to the problem. At the same time, she took the opportunity to point out that improvements to the playground and path had not been carried out during the holiday as promised. When illness prevented the caretaker from attending school to light the fires well in advance of the children's arrival, she just got on and lit them herself; and, when consignments of logs, kindling wood or coal failed to arrive on time, she brought the necessary items from home and replaced them when fresh supplies were delivered. When on one occasion the meals for Linton School were inadvertently delivered with those for Lea School, to ensure that the children did not miss their midday meal and go hungry, she loaded them into her car and sped off to Linton and was still back in time for the beginning of afternoon school. On another occasion, in February 1956, she recorded another food delivery mishap with more than a hint of amusement. She stated: 'The bad weather persisted throughout the week so, because of it, the dinner van did not arrive until after one o'clock. By that time the iron rations had been eaten but the children readily ate the proper dinner'.[2]

Miss Gladys Davies
as a young woman
(by kind permission of
Mrs. H. Edwards)

Miss Davies was a strong and immensely practical woman and very little seems to have caused her much disquiet or alarm. She was well known as a firm disciplinarian who brooked no nonsense from anyone. No doubt, like most head teachers, she had her detractors, but she seems to have had the children's best interests at heart and appears to have been held in great esteem, even by those villagers who coyly admit to having received a well-earned smacked bottom from her. In 1961, on 1 May, Miss Davies wrote in her logbook: 'I have today completed 26 years service at this school and have given notice to terminate that service at the end of term.'[3] She left the school house and retired to a new bungalow she had had built in Hoovers Lane, where she enjoyed a long and energetic retirement. In the early 1990s she was still driving her car and cheerily waved to anyone at the school gate as she drove past. Later she moved to a house in Smallbrook Road in Ross and latterly to a very comfortable retirement home only a short distance away. In 1997, as a mark of the respect she inspired, a party was held in the new village hall at Lea to celebrate her ninetieth birthday, and friends and many former pupils from far and wide gathered there to greet her.

In late Victorian times there appears to have been a generally accepted notion that in rural parishes, such as the Lea, there were usually three confessors: the rector, the doctor and the headmaster, but not necessarily in that order. These were the key people whose education, social standing and overlapping circles of knowledge and influence in parish affairs marked them out as individuals who could give sound advice and whose discretion would be assured. In 1935, when Miss Davies was appointed as headmistress of the school, this notion remained almost untouched, which meant that in the rural setting the head teacher's role in the village community assumed, in some respects, a far greater significance than that of his or her counterparts in the town or city, where people were less well known and it was easier to sustain a more anonymous existence. This was particularly so in the case of a church-aided school because, on appointment, the head teacher accepted the importance of the church's teachings and his or her role in that

Probably Miss Davies's retirement day in 1961.
Immediately behind her is Miss E.M. Jones, assistant teacher since 1941,
and on the extreme left is Mrs. E. Humphrys, lunch-time supervisor for 31 years.
The Revd. H.S. Whatley is in the back row.
(By kind permission of Mrs. M. Melhuish)

*Miss Glady Davies, Headmistress of Lea School from 1935 to 1961, at her ninetieth
birthday party at Lea Village Hall. The top picture shows her with the late
Mr. George Melhuish, former school governor and chairman of governors. Mr. Ron Ablett
is in the background. (By kind permission of Mrs. H. Edwards)*

teaching. The church and the school were central to Miss Davies's life and, as diocesan reports have shown, she was extremely conscientious in preparing her charges for confirmation. Miss Davies was a regular worshipper at the church of St. John the Baptist, just across the road from the school and is remembered for her clear and expressive delivery of epistles, lessons and prayers. She was an astute observer of the world and during her long life witnessed many social changes and saw two generations of her pupils mature and have families of their own. She was the last head teacher to live at the school house, so, when she left, after a quarter of a century at the school, it was the end of an era.

Chapter 12
The Post-War Baby-Boomers Come of Age

In 1960, most adolescents left school at 15 and, since employment opportunities were quite plentiful at that time, they either entered a trade apprenticeship for a period of five or seven years, or were quickly absorbed into the adult labour market. The notion of the 'teenager' who had an assumed right to test parental patience to the limit and flout authority in general, in the arrogant or naive expectation of a wide margin of tolerance and leniency, had yet to evolve. In most cases, youngsters left school as children on one day and, just a few days later, were employed as adults, with very few allowances made for those who failed to achieve the required transformation quickly and successfully. By the mid-1960s, however, when the children of the post-war baby boom came of age, society was changing rapidly and it was a good time to be young and free. The older generations looked on aghast at what they perceived as lax morals and generally poor standards of behaviour amongst the young and, in their disquiet, were quite convinced that the youngsters' antics would soon mire a once proud nation in the depths of depravity. Despite their fears, however, Britain achieved notable successes in sport, science and the arts, with London leading the way as the fashion capital of the world. The 1960s witnessed a social revolution led by the young who were defiantly determined and hugely successful in casting off the restraints of the past. In some respects, authority would never be viewed in quite the same way again.

It was in this unsettled and, for some people, troubled climate that change came to Lea School. In 1961, Miss Gladys Davies embarked on her long retirement and her successor, Mr. Gwynfor Evans, possibly the first headmaster in the school's history, took up his appointment and remained in post until he retired in the summer of 1981. Mr. Evans lived in his own house in Ross, so the vacant school house was let to Mr. and Mrs. Ron Ablett, who lived there for 43 years before moving to a new home in Ross. Their long association with the school served to sustain an interesting continuity with the past, because Mrs. Kath Ablett's father had attended Lea School and she herself had been a pupil of both Mrs. Carter and Miss Davies, and retained many pleasant recollections of those times.

Miss Davies clearly earned a great deal of loyalty from her staff because in 1961, when Mr. Evans became head teacher, Mrs. Ablett was employed as cleaner-in-charge, a post she fulfilled diligently and conscientiously for 27 years. His assistant teacher, Miss

E.M. Jones – later followed by Mrs. Peggy Luker and then Mrs. Iris Pearson – had been Miss Davies's loyal infant teacher since 1941, and Mrs. E. Humphrys, who served and supervised the school meals in the Rectory Room, remained at her post for a very commendable 31 years. In addition, since there was still some emphasis placed on the importance of the girls learning needlework, Mrs. Aspinall, and later Mrs. N. Parker, Mrs. Elliot and Mrs. Sendall, attended school each week to give a needlework lesson, and also did general supply teaching when the need arose.

Mr. Evans was a regular worshipper at Lea Church, sang in the choir for many years and, like his predecessors, was assiduous in sustaining the mutually beneficial bond between church and school. There were services, either in church or in school, for Ash Wednesday, Easter, Ascension Day, Harvest Festival and Mothering Sunday, and at Christmas there were Nativity plays and carol services in the Rectory Room. There were also special assemblies to

Mr. G. Evans, Headmaster
1961-1981
(School Collection)

mark St. George's Day and, interestingly, Commonwealth Day, 24 May, which in former times was celebrated as Empire Day. The records indicate, too, that Mr. Evans attended education conferences at Church House in Gloucester as well as the annual service for the Gloucester Diocesan Teachers' Association. He clearly took his obligations as head teacher of a church-aided school very seriously.

He also did everything he could to keep the school open, even in the most adverse weather conditions. The winter of 1962-1963 was the most severe since 1947. Heavy snow and plunging temperatures at the beginning of the year caused chaos, and schools were instructed to remain closed. Mr. Evans visited the school almost daily, despite the terrible road conditions, to monitor the situation. He acknowledged in the school log book the sterling work done by Mr. and Mrs. Ablett in keeping the school warm, preventing pipes from freezing and clearing the paths of snow. The bitterly cold weather continued, but the school opened as planned on 24 January, with 25 of the 30 children then on the roll present for lessons. Plunging temperatures continued; the outside toilets became blocked with ice and unusable; at times water pipes were frozen underground; and the water supply was off and on and off again for the next six weeks. Many schools would have been closed again, but Mr. Evans carried water for essential needs from the Rectory Room and, when the pipes there were frozen, from the rectory. On several occasions, a local farmer helped out by delivering water to the school in churns. It was not until the first week of March that the thaw began in earnest, and then more burst pipes were discovered, but, no doubt to the annoyance of some of its pupils, Lea School remained open.

In the autumn of 1963, the Revd. H.L. Whatley, a conscientious visitor to the school since his appointment to the parish in July 1949, gave up his living at the Lea to assume the incumbency of Colwall. The school log book suggests that he had been assiduous in his routine of delivering religious-instruction lessons and, in particular, his guiding of the older children in their learning and understanding of the Catechism. He also took his leave of Aston Ingham and curiously, in doing so he severed a previously unbroken line of Whatleys at Aston Ingham rectory which stretched back to the arrival in the parish of the Revd. Charles Whatley in 1785. His successor to both parishes was the Revd. W.B. Harrison, who was equally diligent in attending school to give his weekly lesson. Mr. Evans noted in his log book that he attended both his installation service, conducted by the Bishop of Gloucester in October 1964 and, sadly, just five years later in October 1969, his funeral at Aston Ingham church. The Revd. Harrison was succeeded in the autumn of 1970 by the Revd. H.S. Laws, who lived first at Aston Ingham rectory and later at the Lea.

The 1960s witnessed an expansion of primary-school activities outside the classroom, with the introduction of local music and drama festivals, inter-school football, netball, hockey and rounders matches, weekly swimming lessons at Glewstone Court, and cycling proficiency training, all of which Mr. Evans appears to have embraced and encouraged. In February 1965 the school received a very favourable general inspection report, and in the years that followed, a steady stream of students from Hereford Teacher Training College were placed at Lea for teaching practice and assessment, which might also be seen as an indicator that the school was doing well. This judgement was further reinforced when the school received a very positive report from the Revd. Seacome, who inspected the school for the Diocese of Gloucester in July 1972. He was clearly delighted with what he saw, and no doubt his report pleased Mr. Evans, the school managers and also the Revd. Laws, who was present throughout the visit. The Revd. Seacome wrote: 'My visit to this school was most pleasant and stimulating. The children conducted their own assembly which was impressive for the exceptional quality of the singing with the unexpected inclusion of a second part. This is indicative of skilful direction and a lively response from the children themselves. Despite the handicap of an outdated building the children are in excellent hands and this shows itself in the quality of the work they do and the encouragement they get. Needless to say a happy atmosphere prevails'.[1] Mr. Evans was clearly well-regarded by the Diocese of Gloucester as well as the School Managers.

It must therefore have come as something of a hammer blow when, just a few years later, falling rolls raised the ominous spectre of closure. In the 1960s and the 1970s many small rural communities were confronted with the same problem, and most fought tooth and nail to defeat any such proposals. Few issues were likely to unite village politics more than a threat to the school because everyone knew only too well that when a village lost its school the nature of its society changed; generations of tradition were lost and the real focus for the future of village life was almost irrevocably impaired. By the late 1970s, Lea School had been in existence for almost 120 years, and the children of some local families had attended lessons there for three or four generations. The thought that it might be closed was unthinkable, and something had to be done. In October 1977 at a well-attended parish meeting, the issue was discussed and an Action Committee was formed to campaign against and defeat any suggestion that Lea School should close. The committee, led by Mr. Dick Cole, included: Mr. Mann, Mr. Allan, Mrs. Turner, Mrs. Pearson, Mr. and Mrs. Breeze, Mrs. Robinson, Mr. and Mrs. Stretch, Mrs. Rees and Mr. Evans, the headmaster. Their sterling efforts and those of their supporters were, of course, successful, but the spectre of closure had not gone away completely. It continued to lurk menacingly in the shadows for some years. In May 1981, when Mr. Evans announced that he would be retiring at the end of the summer term, there were just 23 children on the roll. In July he noted that his successor would be Mrs. E.E. Bevan and that her staff would be: Mrs. I. Pearson, assistant teacher; Mrs. K. Ablett, caretaker; Mrs. M. Cole, dining assistant; and Mrs. Rees, children's lunch supervisor. Sadly, Mr. Evans's retirement was not to be a long and happy one. He died suddenly just three weeks later, on 16 August, whilst on holiday.

Mrs. Bevan, the new head teacher, already knew the area well because she had previously taught at Weston-under-Penyard, and lived at Ryeford, almost midway between the two villages. She was introduced to the 23 children in her charge on the first morning of the autumn term by Mr. George Melhuish, at morning assembly. Mr. Melhuish was a loyal supporter of the school for many years, fostering its links with the church as a governor, as the Official Correspondent, as a parent, as a regular worshipper and a member of the church choir and, in 1981, as the Chairman of Governors. At lunch time, the Revd. Ronnie Hambleton, parish priest since the retirement of the Revd. H.S. Laws in 1978, also called in to wish everyone a good term, and so began a new phase in the school's history. These were indeed changing times, because it was at about this time that the school's long and fruitful association with the Diocese of Gloucester came to an end, when the ecclesiastical parish of the Lea was transferred to the Diocese of Hereford. The school soon found a new friend, however, in the Diocesan Director of Education, Mr. Tristram Jenkin, a constant ally whose support and protection was to be vital in the school's success and development for nearly two decades.

The autumn term proceeded well, but preparations for Christmas were severely disrupted as the weather declined sharply, and early snows heralded one of the hardest winters on record. Early on the morning of Friday 11 December, Mrs. Bevan set out from Ryeford in heavy snow to walk to school, but soon after her arrival blizzard conditions ensued and the school was closed. Those children who had arrived were sent home with their parents and later, some who had arrived alone were taken home by Mrs. Bevan's son in his Landrover. The heavy snow continued throughout the weekend and the police advised people not to travel because more blizzards were forecast for the next few days. The school remained closed because the main road running through the village had been closed to traffic on Sunday afternoon and, although opened for single track driving the next day, two stranded lorries completely blocked the entrance to the school drive and the electricity supply was cut off for some 30 hours. Mr. and Mrs. Ablett came to the rescue again and managed to keep a pathway clear from the school gates to the classrooms. The school reopened with just enough time to practise for the carol service and the Nativity play which was planned for a church service on 29 December and to enjoy the school Christmas party. The blizzards returned early in the New Year and the school was closed again until a thaw began on 17 January. With the combined snow-clearing efforts of Mr. and Mrs. Ablett, Mr. and Mrs. Bevan and their son, the school was opened the next day. It had been a testing first winter.

Despite the trials of a punishing winter, and although the number of children on roll remained low and the school's long-term survival was still uncertain, the governors sustained a positive outlook and pursued building plans for the future. Governor and County Councillor Mrs. Eunice Saunders convened a site meeting to discuss with the Diocesan Architect, Mr. Nigel Dees, the possibility of bringing the school's outbuildings under one roof to make better use of the available space, discussions which ultimately resulted in a larger scale development several years later. At the same time, a Parent and Teacher Association initiated by another governor, Mr. Dick Cole, was busy with a variety of fund-raising events. The funds were essentially to help to pay the cost of the coach to take the children to Ross for their weekly swimming lessons, but later included provision for some extra general purchases and to subsidise transport for other educational visits.

An important element of Mrs. Bevan's teaching philosophy was to take the children out to visit interesting places to engender enthusiasm for class projects, to broaden their horizons, and to stimulate their curiosity about the world. The annual visit to Hereford Cathedral for the schools' Ascension Day service, for example, was usually combined with a visit to the world-famous chained library, the cathedral treasury or some other place of interest on the way back to school. In addition, there were visits to other churches, abbeys, castles, museums, heritage centres, water mills, music recitals and plays, as well as walks to local places of interest. These included a visit to Eccleswall Court to look at the site of a Norman castle, a trip to Castle End Farm to observe the wildlife in and around the lake, and an annual spring visit to Rock Farm for the infant class to see the

Mrs. Kath Ablett is on the left, and next to her is Mrs. Diane Brice.
On the right is Mrs. E.E. Bevan, headmistress (School Collection)

new-born lambs. Similarly, people with interesting skills such as violin playing or spinning were invited to demonstrate them, and older members of the community were persuaded to talk to the children about their own time as pupils at the school.

By the autumn of 1985, the number of children on the roll had risen to 36, which meant that Mrs. Diane Brice, previously appointed on a part-time basis, could now be employed as a full-time teacher. Mrs. Rose Savidge became School Secretary. The numbers were predicted to rise to the low 40s by the beginning of the spring term, so a special meeting was called for the governors to consider the need for more classroom space. After some discussion between the governors and the Diocesan Director of Education, Mr. Tristram Jenkin, the diocese supplied a demountable classroom to provide additional teaching space until funds could be made available for a major remodelling of the school. The delivery of the classroom caused some excitement; the main road had to be closed and the traffic diverted whilst sections of the new building were hoisted into place. The classroom was soon occupied by Mrs. Brice and the junior class, Mrs. Bevan and the infants moved into the original 1859 classroom, and the small infant room was made available so that the school doctor, dentist, nurse, child psychologist and special-needs teachers could work without disrupting the school's general teaching routine. This was a great boon to everyone, and suggested that the school's long-term future was looking much more secure. The spectre of closure had been driven further into the shadows.

It was largely due to the persistence of Mrs. Eunice Saunders that the remodelling, to provide an extra permanent classroom, a small kitchen, a head teacher's office, staff room and new toilet facilities, finally began in January 1988. It proved to be something of a trial to everyone, because teaching had to continue around the building site and it was not until almost the end of the summer term that the work was completed. By that time, interviews had taken place to select a new head teacher for the autumn term, and Miss Elizabeth James was appointed. Mrs. Bevan would have happily continued to teach well into the future but unfortunately regulations are regulations, and retirement beckoned. Sadly, Miss James was not able to enjoy the new development for very long, because in the summer term of her second year she had to relinquish her post on health grounds.

On the last day of the summer term Mr. Jenkin visited the school to thank Mrs. Bevan for her hard work and good stewardship of the school and also to wish her a happy retirement. She had served the school and its pupils well for seven years, had sustained the links between church and school as faithfully as her predecessors, and, with the help of loyal and determined governors, had successfully steered it through the dark days of near closure to the bright days of renewal and expansion. In conversation at her home in August 2009, she stated unequivocally that she loved teaching, loved being with the children and loved being head teacher of Lea School. It seems rather unjust that having endured the anxieties of teaching throughout the building process, Mrs. Bevan could not enjoy the new buildings for even a few years. As it transpired, there was a curious twist to all that had happened because, with rising numbers of children on the roll and the advent of the new National Curriculum, within just a few years the problem of space was to become an issue once more.

Conclusion

The history of elementary education in Victorian and Edwardian times suggests that the children's attendance at school was often impeded by a number of stubbornly entrenched problems: the high levels of rural poverty; the importance of children's earnings in the family income; serious epidemics of dangerous childhood diseases; inadequate outdoor clothing and footwear for winter walks to school; poorly heated and overcrowded school buildings; and the frequent resignations of teachers who became dispirited by their pupils' frequent absences and disappointingly poor progress. The most intractable problem, however, was the enduring conflict of interests between those members of the community who endeavoured to keep the children at their lessons in school and those who saw no reason to educate the poor because they wanted them to be available to labour in the fields. It is reasonable to suggest that progress in rural schools depended greatly on the influence and attitudes of enlightened, prominent people such the Colchester family and the unwavering support of men like the Revd. William David Hall and later the Revd. Charles Buee. In the case of Lea School, it might be supposed, therefore, that the influence of these men created an ethos in which teachers like Mrs. Elizabeth King, Mrs. A.J. Edkins and Miss Elizabeth Watkins were content to give long and faithful service because pupil absence was not a particular issue compared with other schools.

There can be little doubt, though, that the older children spent some of their lesson time working in nearby fields in order to help to fill the labour shortage created by the mass call to arms in 1914. The nation's priority then was survival, and educational reform had to wait until better days. The wait proved to be a long one because when the armistice was declared in 1918, England was exhausted and almost bankrupt. The peace brought financial chaos and years of austerity, to be followed by another world war. Mrs. Edkins, Mrs. Carter and Miss Davies had, therefore, to make do with the educational resources available to them, and it was not until the late 1940s that the long awaited reorganisation of elementary schools into primary and secondary schools began to take place. The 1950s and the 1960s were years of recovery and rebuilding and the firm establishment of the dual system of grammar schools and secondary modern schools, while the 1970s witnessed the gradual progress towards comprehensive education.

The reforms of the late 1980s and the 1990s generated a surging tide of change which swept over almost every aspect of primary education and left many of the most experienced teachers concerned that the spontaneity so valued in the teaching of young children had been too greatly curtailed by the highly prescriptive nature of the new National Curriculum. This was perhaps most keenly felt in rural areas, where it was considered appropriate and normal to take an interest in traditional village events or respond to unexpected local happenings. A spontaneous visit to see new-born lambs, inspect the exposed roots of a great oak which had been blown down in an overnight gale, or collect frog spawn from a shallow sandy brook nearby, might all be valuable activities for increasing vocabulary and improving language development, as well as stimulating ideas for story writing or drawing and painting. When interesting and exciting things happen, small children want to see them and be involved immediately, and thoughtful teachers use these enthusiasms to good effect. Some things simply cannot be planned or timetabled in advance – and next week is too late. It was in the midst of these manifold and slightly bewildering changes that I took up my appointment as head teacher of Lea School in the autumn of 1990.

The one constant influence in all this change, despite changing fortunes and markedly fewer regular worshippers, was the church. This point was made manifest to me soon after the close of school one sunny, September afternoon when Mrs. Alma Urquhart, the Clerk to the Governors, presented me with two copies of my new contract of employment. They were printed on thick glossy paper, and had to be signed by both head teacher and clerk in the presence of each other and a witness. Although I had taught in other Church of England schools and, as a communicant, accepted the church's teaching, I had never before taught in a church-aided school, nor had I previously encountered that degree of formality in accepting contractual obligations. Soon all was revealed. One particular clause drew my attention to the fact that in signing the contract I agreed to give or to supervise the giving of religious instruction in accordance with the doctrines of the Church of England and also that I would never do anything contrary to the Church-of-England character of the school's foundation. In a church-

aided school the church has long established rights and responsibilities. In the case of Lea School, the head teacher's contract of employment is with the school's Board of Governors and the Diocese of Hereford. The contracts were signed and witnessed by assistant teacher Mrs. Diane Brice, and I became the latest in a long line of head teachers charged with the duty to uphold the teachings of the church and, indirectly, to perpetuate the vision of the school's enlightened founder and benefactor, the Revd. William David Hall. At that point in time, of course, I had never heard of him.

The previous summer term had been an unsettling time for everyone, and with several changes of staff, the school was greatly in need

Mrs. Sue Sherwood, school caretaker

of a period of steady routine and restorative calm. At the beginning of the autumn term there were two full-time teachers, myself and Mrs. Diane Brice, assisted by Mrs. Helen Banks, who taught mornings only. The support staff were: Mrs. Sue Sherwood, caretaker; Mrs. Ruth Howells, road crossing patrol; Mrs. Fenella Roberts, school secretary and lunch-time assistant; Mrs. Grace Rushworth, lunch-time supervisor; and the late Mrs. Sylvia Gleed, who was a classroom assistant.

The years of my period in office, 1990-1997, were to a large extent shaped by the introduction of the National Curriculum, which set down in considerable detail the nine subjects to be taught to almost all children from 5 years of age; admission policies; pupil assessment; the controversial testing of 7 and 11 year-olds; and local authority delegation of budget control and financial responsibility to individual schools. In the autumn of 1990, however, these changes were still in their infancy, long established notions and methods of teaching primary school children continued to prevail, and as the new term progressed, the school settled into a productive routine of lessons, projects, church festivals, regular services and village events.

A wildlife project, for example, drew on the knowledge and expertise of a member of the local 'Badger Watch' group. A study of the Ancient Greeks included a presentation from a teacher who had been present during the sea trials of a modern, full-sized replica of a Greek trireme, the fighting ship which had assured Athenian naval supremacy over other city states. And an India-Day project drew comparisons between local village life and life in a rural village in India, as well as providing opportunities to try on Indian clothes and sample Indian food. There were cycling proficiency lessons, orienteering exercises and the usual sporting fixtures for football, netball and rounders matches with neighbouring schools. The rector, the Revd. Ronnie Hambleton, followed steadfastly in the footsteps of his predecessors. He visited school to give weekly lessons in religious instruction, officiated at a church assembly every Thursday morning and, in his own quiet and gentle manner, encouraged the children in celebrating their own Harvest Festival service, as well as their performance of Nativity plays and sketches for Mothering Sunday. A positive mood prevailed, the school attracted support from many sources beside members of the clergy, teachers, parents and governors, and the following spring brought pleasing and reassuring observations from one of Her Majesty's Inspectors. He was very pleased with the quality of the teaching, the spontaneity of the children's responses in their class discussions, the quality and quantity of their work and the pleasant way in which they played together at break times.

As the implementation of the National Curriculum began to take effect, however, it soon exposed the inadequate nature of some school buildings. Some small schools began to struggle with the problem of providing sufficient working space for practical experiments in science, technology and design technology and, in the absence of a school hall, the difficulty of fulfilling all the requirements of the physical education syllabus. In this respect, the Lea children were to benefit greatly from the completion of the splendid new village hall in the summer of 1991. It was attractively sited on open farm land behind the school which afforded a very easy passage between the two buildings. In an agreement between the Village Hall Trustees and the County Education Department,

Lea Village Hall

several two-hour blocks of time were made available for the school's use each week and in addition the county provided the necessary equipment for the building to be used as a school gymnasium as and when required. This development was very timely, because the school's population was growing and admission lists for succeeding terms suggested that the increase would continue well into the future.

In September 1990 there were just 39 children on the roll, but a year later the figure had risen to 52 and would shortly exceed the school's official capacity of 55 places. In December 1991, however, the Diocesan Director of Education, Mr. Jenkin, arranged for a new demountable classroom – funded 85% by the Department for Education and 15% by the Diocese of Hereford in accordance with the requirements of church-aided status – to be delivered and erected in readiness for the beginning of the summer term in 1992, when the number of children on the roll was expected to be greater than the school's designated capacity. The arrival of the new classroom increased capacity to 84 places, but in November that year, County Councillor and school governor Mrs. Eunice Saunders cut the first sod of a new Gloucestershire Housing Association development of 40 houses which was well within the school's catchment area, and suggested that the recently increased capacity might soon be absorbed once again. Indeed, the children living on the new estate, known as Rudhall View, began to arrive at school in September 1993, and just before Christmas that year a second demountable classroom was delivered. Thus it was that the little school whose future had been in such perilous doubt just a few years earlier survived to become a flourishing four-class school and, most importantly, the sinister spectre of closure had been driven so far into the shadows that it was no longer felt to be a threat.

At this point, although immediate difficulties with classroom accommodation had been resolved, the governors started to focus their attention on the need for new permanent buildings, and to that end began in earnest to hold exploratory talks with officials from both the County Education Department and the Diocese of Hereford. The central issue affecting future development was the lack of available land. The playground was now too small for the number of children using it but could not be extended because it was bounded by school buildings on two sides and by the village-hall drive and the school field on the other two sides. The situation was further complicated by the fact that the school field was held in private ownership and the school's lease on it was due to expire early in the twenty-first century, so time was of the essence. If an entirely new school was to be built on a fresh site, the Diocesan Director of Education could apply for an 85% grant from the government but, in accordance with church-aided status, the Board of Governors would have to acquire the other 15% which meant raising many tens of thousands of pounds, without any regular source of income. This was a daunting task but to their great credit the governors did not flinch from the challenge, but embarked on a programme of fund-raising events. The vision of an entirely new school, however, appeared to be quite some years away.

In the summer of 1992, the Revd. Ronnie Hambleton said farewell to the Lea and retired to a parish on the Isle of Skye where he could continue with some church duties but also have time to indulge his love of sailing. He was followed in January 1993 by the Revd. Tim Alban Jones who also played a very full part in the life of the school as a priest, a governor and a teacher. He had arrived at a very interesting time in the school's history. The number of children on the roll had recently doubled and although this had assured its future, the increase in numbers brought with it some settling-in problems which persisted throughout the autumn term of 1993 and were not really resolved until the following spring. Gradually, however, the rivalries subsided, an air of calm returned, and in May 1994, despite the upheavals of the previous two terms, there was very reassuring news. Inspectors from the County Education Department carried out a three-year review of the school's performance and progress and, apart from a few minor points, their findings were both positive and pleasing. The school was in good heart and its Church-of-England ethos remained strong. It was still fulfilling its founder's intentions.

The teaching staff were well aware, however, that in large towns and cities the pupils of some Church of England Schools come from a number of different religious backgrounds which allows them to foster friendships with children of other faiths through the normal daily interactions of lessons and play. In small rural schools, the circumstances are usually rather different because, although they adhere to the National Curriculum requirements for the study of comparative religions, their countryside locations afford few opportunities for their pupils to meet children from different environments, backgounds and faiths. It was with this reality in mind that exchange visits were arranged between an infant class from Lea School and one from Hatherley Road Infant School in Gloucester. The schools' environments could hardly be more different, one being set amongst city buildings and the other surrounded by green fields.

The first visit, arranged by Mrs. Iris Calderbank and Miss Louise James, took place in March 1995. For some of the Lea children, the bewildering walk through long city streets to visit a mosque was an education in itself, and almost certainly their first real

Lea School 1996
Adults (left to right): Miss Lucy Towle, Mrs. Jeannie Sherwood, Mrs. Anne Kirby,
the late Mrs. Sylvia Gleed, Mrs. Diane Brice, Mr. John Powell, Mrs. Iris Calderbank,
Mrs. Helen Banks, Mrs. Susie Williams and Mrs. Margaret Hay (School Collection)

experience of an urban environment. At the mosque, they were warmly greeted and were able to see and experience many aspects of religious observance which previously they had seen only in books or on film. After lunch with their new companions they took part in a school assembly and returned to the Lea with much to tell everyone the next day. In July, the parallel class of children from Hatherley Road Infant School made a return visit to experience a day exploring the countryside. For some of them it was clearly a very new experience. Whilst most of them immediately enjoyed the freedom of the fields, others were a little overawed and initially unable to cope with all the space. Their walk took them first to the Westlea Animal Rescue Centre and then on to the local riding stables where, blessed by a glorious day, they ate their picnic lunch. Then, after pony rides for everyone, they walked back across the fields to school, tired but happy with their day in the country – and the visits have continued ever since.

As the school evolved and grew, the staff grew and changed too. Mrs. Iris Calderbank and Miss Lucy Towle were appointed to the teaching staff to join Mrs. Brice, Mrs. Banks and myself, and Mrs. Anne Kirby and Miss Louise James gave the school a great deal of valuable voluntary teaching time, and also provided supply cover when necessary. The support staff included Mrs. Sylvia Gleed, Mrs. Jean Lacey, Mrs. Jackie Byard, Mrs. Susie Williams, Mrs. Betty Rigotti, Mrs. Sue Sherwood, Mrs. Heather Puttick, Mrs. Jeannie Sherwood and Mrs. Margaret Hay, who followed Mrs. Fenella Roberts as school secretary. I was most fortunate in having good staff and I shall always be grateful to them for giving so freely of their own time and for the thoughtfulness, industry and spirit of co-operation which did so much to foster the school's progress and many successes. I am similarly appreciative of the school governors for their enthusiasm, loyalty and courtesy.

I sometimes used to hear other head teachers bewailing the fact that they had difficult governors who made decisions contrary to their advice, but despite some lively discussions at board meetings, under the thoughtful leadership of the Revd. Ronnie Hambleton and later Mrs. Eunice Saunders and Mrs. Margaret Watson I never experienced such difficulties and the Lea School Governors were always very supportive. The members of the school's Parent and Teacher Association also worked very hard in support of school events and in raising funds for numerous items, not least a very welcome new piano, and I shall be eternally grateful to them too. Just before Christmas 1996, I took the decision to take early retirement in order to concentrate on 19th-century Poor Law research, and was awarded the degree of Doctor of Philosophy in 2001.

I took my leave at Easter 1997 and, confident in the knowledge that the school would be safe and secure in the capable hands of my loyal deputy, Mrs. Di Brice, I embarked on a six-week ramble around Europe before settling down to complete my research and write my thesis. My successor, Mr. Colin Howard, took up his post at the beginning of the autumn term and a new and eventful phase of the school's history ensued. The school house became vacant when Mr. and Mrs. Ablett moved to Ross and, after several short lettings, it was decided that with a little remodelling, it could be incorporated into the school to provide much needed office and storage space, as well as a larger staff room and a staff kitchen. In July 1998 the school received a very good OFSTED report and, in its edition of 23 July, the *Ross Gazette* quoted the extremely satisfying words with which the inspectors began: 'Lea C of E Primary School is a good school with a strong, community ethos. It has many strengths of which it can be justifiably proud including high quality teaching and good links with the village.' This was a report of which everyone connected with the school, past and present, could be proud, not least its oldest surviving head teacher, Miss Gladys Davies.

Miss Davies remained bright and alert well into old age, and her interest in her old school continued undimmed. In early 1998, for example, in the company of her almost equally aged colleague, Mrs. Nora Parker, she accepted an invitation to take tea with class three juniors to talk about the school in former times. Sadly, in the autumn of that year she died at the ripe old age of 91, but she had not finished with the school yet, because under the terms of her will, the bulk of her estate was to be divided between Lea Church and Lea School. The governors were still endeavouring to raise their 15% share of the cost of the proposed new school, and with Miss Davies's bequest, the required sum was almost within their grasp. This gave new impetus to the governors' fund raising and, under the determined leadership of Mrs. Margaret Watson – a stalwart governor for almost a quarter of a century – a new school was almost within sight.

The site chosen for the new buildings was a secluded field just behind the new village hall and only 150 yards or so from the original Victorian school. The choice of this location created an unexpected, but interesting, link with the past, because the provision of pedestrian access through a side gate from the village-hall grounds means that the children pass the Revd. William David Hall's school – now transformed into houses – as they walk to and from school or go to church. It was several more years

Lea School News.

Monday 1st June 1998. Edition 1.

The Interview

By Gemma

On Thursday 21st May Class 3 interviewed some people who came to Lea School when they were little. Some were teachers. The photo is of Mrs Parker and myself. Jackie Byard said they had desks instead of drawers. I would like desks instead too. They were unlucky because if they need the toilet desperately they had to go all the way outside. Miss Davis had been teaching as a head for over 30 yrs. When they came to Lea school the field was used for a paddock for animals.

Mrs. Nora Parker, aged 87, taking tea with Class 3 in June 1998
(By kind permission of Mrs. Jenny Hatton)

before the new school was complete and ready for occupation, but the long wait proved to be well worth while because the architect, Jonathan Price, and his team had created an attractive teaching and learning environment in a secure and beautiful setting of which everyone might be proud. It was without doubt a source of enormous satisfaction for all those people who had laboured in different ways to achieve its completion. The new buildings include four classrooms with views across games and recreational areas and on the other side, internal windows look on

The last day at the old school.
Left to right: Mrs. Linda Townsend, Miss Louise James,
Mrs. Diane Brice, Mrs. Margaret Hay, John Powell
and Mrs. Iris Calderbank

to a large craft area and beyond that there is a computer suite and a well appointed hall which provides for music, drama and physical education lessons and school assemblies. At one end of the hall a long, narrow and distinctly church-like window has been completed with a stained-glass depiction of the 'tree of life' in memory of the late Miss Gladys Davies (1907-1998) (see rear cover), whose gift greatly advanced the building of a splendid new school.

The official opening of the new school took place on 5 November 2004, and was performed by the Revd. Tim Alban Jones, who travelled from his new Cambridgeshire parish for the occasion. It was, however, a delighted Chairman of Governors, Mrs. Margaret Watson – the driving force behind the campaign for new buildings – who cut the tape to admit the children for their first day's lessons on 10 June 2004. That was a day to be savoured and remembered.

The last day of teaching at the old school, Thursday 27 May 2004, did not pass without celebration, but it was a curious day of mixed emotions for everyone. At the kind suggestion of Mrs. Helen Banks, I was invited back to teach for the last morning, and I was very happy to do so, but I was also well aware that it really was the end of an era. In the afternoon the school was opened to parents, past pupils, villagers and former members of staff to take a last look round, and many people took the opportunity to visit. Afterwards, they were invited to take tea at tables set up in the playground. On a pleasantly warm summer afternoon, it was a fitting and convivial end to the school's role at the centre of village life for almost 150 years.

In recent times it has been fashionable to mock the Victorians for holding what later generations have perhaps justifiably perceived as bewilderingly hypocritical social attitudes, but it cannot be denied that they were energetically inventive in industry

Dorothy and Marjory Lane.
(Kind permission of Mrs. Pearl Ager, Marjorie's daughter)

and, as subjects of a queen who was the ruler of the greatest Empire the world had ever known, appear to have been imbued with an enormous confidence in Britain's role and future progress in the world. Their astute political vision of sustaining an Empire of peoples infused with British values and ideals, from whom the mother country might assuredly expect and receive help in times of danger, had proved its wisdom in two world wars.

Despite the dismantling of that Empire in the 1960s and the 1970s, many people throughout the world retain an empathy with their British roots to the present day. During my years as head teacher of Lea School I received a number of interesting letters from Australia, America, Canada and New Zealand, as well as many places in Great Britain, requesting information from or about former pupils, and I always gave their writers as much assistance as possible. Often, requests came from evacuees or their children and the success or failure of such enquiries almost always depended on how the child came to be evacuated.

When a whole class was evacuated, the children's admission records were kept separate from those of the host school and returned to the evacuees' own Local Education Authority when the need for evacuation ended. If, however, a child was evacuated to the area because of a parent's work or was sent privately to stay with relatives or friends for the duration of the war, then his or her details were entered into the host school's records, and in those cases I was sometimes able to assist families with their research.

Occasionally, there were visits from overseas travellers too. In September 1992, for example, a gentleman from Cleveland, Ohio called to see if the school where his father and grandfather had been pupils still existed, and was amazed when he was told he was standing in the actual room where they were taught. In June 1993, two sisters and their husbands, who lived in Canada, called to look at their old school after spending the afternoon visiting Mr. and Mrs. Ablett at the school house. Although the sisters had left the school in 1949, after just a few moments in their old classroom they could pinpoint exactly where they sat and the precise location of Miss Davies's desk. They recalled, too, their long walk from Wigpool in all winds and weathers, and Miss Davies's insistence on absolute punctuality.

In April 2008, the present head teacher, Mrs. Linda Townsend, received an interesting communication from a lady in Western Australia which, in some respects, underlines the notion of an enduring empathy with roots in England. In this case, the writer's mother had fond memories of days spent in Mrs. Carter's class at Lea School. A little research revealed that in the mid-1920s the Lane family lived at Yatton and the children, Dorothy, Marjorie and Timothy, attended the school at Much Marcle. Later they moved to Lea Bailey Cottage at Wigpool, at which point Marjorie and Timothy attended Lea School. An examination of the admissions register clearly indicates in Mrs. Carter's hand that the two children were admitted on 4 July 1927 and, like most youngsters at that time, they left when they were 14 years old. In later years the family left England to start a new life in Australia, and in due course Dorothy and Timothy travelled still further to live in Canada. Marjorie, however, remained in Australia and often talked of her happy days at the Lea. When she left school in the late 1920s each child was presented with a printed card entitled 'On Leaving School' which provided sound advice for living a respectable and fulfilling life. Although a little dated in its wording, in essence that advice remains as valid today as it was 80 years ago. Marjorie's treasured copy, now in the possession of her daughter, Mrs. Pearl Ager, has survived in almost perfect condition, which in itself says much, and underlines an enduring empathy with English roots.

In conclusion, we might pause for a moment to consider what the Revd. William David Hall might think about his school now. It has survived the threat of closure. It continues to be at the centre of village life. It has received good inspection reports. Its Church-of-England ethos remains strong. The children still attend church assembly each week. In short, the vision of this Victorian clergyman has been fulfilled and his school is flourishing. I am sure he would be delighted with its success if he were to know of it – but then perhaps he does.

Bibliography

Taylor, A.J.P., *English History 1914-1945*, Penguin Books Ltd., 1970.

Duff, D., *Queen Mary*, Collins, 1985.

Curtis, A.J., *History of Education in Great Britain*, University Tutorial Press, 6th Ed., 1965.

Lacey, R., *Royal, Her Majesty Queen Elizabeth II*, Time Warner Paperbacks, 2002.

The Herefordshire Village Book, published jointly by Countryside Books, Newbury and the Herefordshire Federation of Women's Institutes, Hereford, 1989.

Weintraub, S., *Albert Uncrowned King*, John Murray Ltd., 1997.

Hibbert, C., *Queen Victoria*, Harper Collins, 2000.

Ross Gazette.

Papers held at Herefordshire Record Office, Harold Street, Hereford
> Lea Churchwardens' Accounts and Vestry Minutes 1850-1901. HRO Ref. AG52/11.
> Upton Bishop School Log Book. HRO Ref. M43/1.
> Orcop School Log Book. HRO Ref. F62/1
> Hope Mansell School Log Book. HRO Ref. AA100/1.
> Linton Church Seating Plan of 1839. HRO Ref. BM26/4.

Papers in Private Collection
> Lea School Trust Deed dated 1858.
> National Society Grant Deed dated 1873.

Records held at Lea Church
> Parish Registers of Marriages, Baptisms and Burials.
> Lea Church Vestry Minutes dated 1941.

Notes and References

Chapter 1
1. Lea School Trust Deed dated 23.12.1858.
2. National Society Grant Deed dated 03.12.1873.

Chapter 3
1. Orcop School Log Book. HRO Ref. F62/1 May, 1874.
2. Lea Church Vestry Minutes. HRO Ref. AG52/11 04.08.1874.
3. *Ibid.* 14.04.1875.

Chapter 4
1. Orcop School Log Book. HRO Ref. F62/1 30.03.1883.
2. *Ibid.* June, 1884.
3. Upton Bishop School Log Book. HRO M43/1 22.06.1896.
4. Lea Church Vestry Minutes. HRO Ref. AG52/11 19.04.1897.

Chapter 5
1. Taylor, A.J.P., *English History 1914-1945*, p.226.

Chapter 6
1. Lea School Log Book 06.12.1929.
2. *Ibid.* 04.09.1931.
3. *Ibid.* 11.09.1930.
4. *Ibid.* 14.12.1934.
5. *Ibid.* 17.01.1935.

Chapter 7
1. Lea School Log Book 08.02.1937.
2. *Ibid.* 27.03.1928.
3. *Ibid.* 24.11.1933.
4. *Ibid.* 09.02.1937.
5. *Ibid.*
6. *Ibid.* 26.05.1938.

Chapter 8
1. Lea School Log Book 01.09.1939.
2. *Ibid.* 17.10.1939.
3. *Ibid.* 08.12.1939.

Chapter 9
1. Lea Church Vestry Minutes Feb. 1941.
2. *Ibid.*
3. Lea School Log Book 27.04.1939.
4. *Ibid.* 20.12.1939.
5. *Ibid.* 29.05.1940.
6. *Ibid.* 05.02.1941.
7. *Ibid.* 01.08.1941.
8. *Ibid.*
9. *Ibid.* 10.08.1942.
10. *Ibid.* 16.03.1943.
11. *Ibid.* 14.05.1943.
12. *Ibid.* 22.10.1943.
13. *Ibid.*
14. *Ibid.* 25.07.1944.

Chapter 10
1. Lea School Log Book 29.01.1947.
2. *Ibid.* 10.02.1947.
3. *Ibid.* 13.02.1947.
4. *Ibid.* 05.03.1947.
5. *Ibid.* 06.03.1947.
6. *Ibid.* 21.03.1947.
7. *Ibid.* 15.09.1947.
8. *Ibid.* 15.10.1948.

Chapter 11
1. Lea School Log Book 08.02.1952.
2. *Ibid.* 03.02.1956.
3. *Ibid.* 01.05.1961.

Chapter 12
1. Lea School Log Book 09.03.1973.

Index

Page numbers in italics indicate illustrations